COACHING
RUGBY 7s

COACHING
RUGBY 7s

MARCUS BLACKBURN

A & C BLACK • LONDON

For my family

Published in 2006 by A & C Black Publishers Ltd
38 Soho Square, London W1D 3HB
www.acblack.com

ISBN-10: 0 7136 7674 4
ISBN-13: 978 0 7136 7674 7

A CIP record for this book is available from the British Library.

A & C Black uses paper produced with elemental chlorine-free pulp, harvested from managed
sustainable forests.

Acknowledgements
Cover photograph © Getty Images
Illustrations by Mark Silver
Textual photographs © Empics

Typeset in Celeste by Palimpsest, Book Production Limited, Polmont, Stirlingshire

Printed and bound in Spain by GraphyCems.

CONTENTS

ACKNOWLEDGEMENTS

There are few coaches who are willing to talk openly about their ideas, especially coaches at the highest level. Fortunately for me, Colin Hillman, former coach of Wales Sevens, is one of them. I am extremely grateful to Colin for sharing his expertise and experience when I was the youngest national coach on the IRB Sevens circuit.

There are probably many undiscovered rugby geniuses in the world, and I am thankful that I have had the fortune to meet one of them – Ricky Horlock. Spending just a short amount of time with Ricky in New Zealand was enough to inspire and enlighten. Huge thanks too to his brother, my great friend Brendan-Ray, for sharing his insights on footwork and never failing to embarrass me in a one-on-one in his backyard!

Thank you to all the players and fellow coaches who openly shared their ideas and allowed me to experiment and develop my own.

Thank you also to Robert Foss and Claire Dunn and everyone at A & C Black who has helped put this project together.

Finally, thank you to my wife Tara for putting up with a husband who spends almost all his time either on a rugby field or at a computer writing this book!

FOREWORD

Sevens has always been a big part of my rugby life. I first played it when I was eight years old at Trimsaran Primary School. From that point on, I continued playing sevens throughout my career and was fortunate enough to take part in some great matches. I played in the famous Dubai Sevens tournament and was also part of a World Sevens team that took on South Africa and played alongside some of the game's greats like David Campese.

To me, the essence of rugby sevens is enjoyment – and this is why the game has so much appeal to children and adults, players and spectators. Sevens gives players much more space to express themselves. Not only does this develop a better appreciation of space – how to create it and how to exploit it – it also makes players more aware defensively in order to cover the extra space on the field. Teamwork and the ability to play to patterns become essential and enhance the enjoyment of the game. Sevens also challenges fitness levels and hones ball-handling skills, making it a great game to play and watch and a perfect platform to develop players for the full 15-a-side game.

The IRB Sevens tournaments are now firmly established on the sporting calendar and some of the most exciting rugby players in the world are being discovered through the sevens game. More and more countries are acknowledging that sevens is an ideal way to develop speed and skills and to expose up-and-coming players to an elite standard of competition. And it is great to see that efforts are being made to develop the game at grassroots level too, as well as in countries where rugby has never really featured as a sport, giving them a chance to compete on the world stage – the Kenyan sevens team is a superb example of a team helping to get the whole country interested in rugby. I was lucky enough to be involved in a memorable trip to Patagonia where we introduced rugby sevens to complete beginners and saw first-hand the enjoyment that the game brings to people from all cultures.

Sevens is a great game and hopefully this book will be enjoyed by all that read it. Long may the sevens game continue to grow and entertain us!

Jonathan Davies MBE
Commentator and former Welsh International

INTRODUCTION

It is almost an injustice to call sevens an *abbreviated* form of rugby. It is an intensive, lightning-paced, pressure-packed version of the game; a spectacle that magnetises millions of people around the world. In sevens, players have *more* opportunities to run, pass, kick, tackle, communicate and make decisions than in other forms of rugby, and all in a fraction of the time.

It is no surprise that all players love sevens. It is also no wonder that sevens has become the vehicle for top rugby nations to develop their stars of the future. With the creation of the IRB Sevens tournaments, the profile and popularity of rugby sevens has soared and it is now deservedly viewed as a game, and big business, in its own right. In terms of a pathway, young players and coaches the world over now have something to aspire to and be inspired by.

I wrote this book because I felt I had something to share, having coached on the IRB Sevens circuit. We are not all fortunate enough to have a Waisale Serevi in our teams, or other special players who can change a game with one step or astound with sheer pace or creative flair, but as a coach you should still be ambitious about producing a successful sevens team. The traditional approach to coaching sevens was to pick the most talented individuals and rely on their brilliance and spontaneity to score tries, and selection was perhaps a bigger concern than the actual preparation of the team. However, this is no longer the case; now the team that is the most organised and best prepared *collectively* will most often be the winning team. This book helps you prepare such a team.

It is no secret that the fitter, faster and stronger players are, the greater contribution they can make to the team and to its success. However, since there is already a wealth of resources on sports and rugby-specific conditioning, this book will focus on the technical and coaching aspects of the game. I should also point out that the book is written with masculine reference just for convenience, and is just as applicable to the women's game as it is to the men's.

The book is effectively an action plan for sevens coaches as well as an insightful guide for players. Part 1 details the plan, while Part 2 presents the drills and practices needed to put the plan into action. Even if the team does not run every pattern or move perfectly, by coaching, encouraging and reinforcing the ideas in this book, you will produce a team of players who have a better appreciation of time and space on the rugby field, a better understanding of how to beat opponents, and a team who work harder off the ball in both attack and defence. You will then be a few steps closer to success.

Good luck in striving for those perfect fourteen minutes!

Marcus Blackburn
May 2006

PART 1
TACTICS

1 PATTERNS OF ATTACK
A GAME OF MOVEMENT

The ability to play with width and speed is the key to successful attack. In sevens, players should aim to occupy the full width of the pitch, effectively positioning themselves in seven imaginary lanes spread equally across the field. This concept is somewhat challenged when contact is made as players will have to move in to support and secure possession, but in general players should aim to use as much of the width of the field as their passing skills allow. It takes discipline to keep this width in attack as players are generally so eager to get their hands on the ball that they move towards it. A common bad habit is 'ball-watching', where players almost become magnetised by the ball and stare at it instead of scanning the defence for opportunities and space to attack. The players furthest out should take on the responsibility of keeping width in the team, but all players need to develop an appreciation of space.

This is a straightforward concept, but it needs to be constantly reinforced. Basically, if the attacking team spread out across the full width of the field, the defenders will either have to follow them and risk becoming isolated, or stand close together and have to drift sideways to cover attacks out wide, leaving themselves vulnerable to changes of direction or being beaten on the outside. Either way, there are opportunities for attack with a widely spread alignment.

'Numbers'

Attack in sevens is not rocket science, but it does involve mathematics. The attacking team will generally be faced with a defensive line of six players, as the defending team will have to play with a sweeper to cover kicks. This gives the attack a simple numerical advantage and forces the six defenders to shift and slide constantly to cover the seven attackers (see figure 1.1). 'Numbers' is a simple call that tells the player in possession of the ball that the defence are stretched and outnumbered. A sense of urgency, as well as quick and accurate passing, is then needed by all players to move the ball in to the space.

A 'numbers' opportunity often arises after contact when the defence are compressed, especially when the attacking team recycle the ball quickly. A long clearing pass away from the tackle situation and a widely spread attacking alignment will stretch the defence further. However, it is not just about moving the ball out to the widest player. Each player, on receiving the ball, should run straight to commit a defender and keep scanning the defence to assess whether the 'Numbers' option is still available.

USE THE NUMBERS TO ACHIEVE OVERLAPS

There is always a numerical advantage in 7s, as most teams employ a sweeper and play with six defenders in the defensive line. If they don't employ a sweeper, the simple option is to kick with an organised chase. The aim is to move the ball quickly enough to the extra man to beat the defence, using a combination of swift passing, straight running and depth in alignment.

| FIGURE 1.1 | NUMBERS |

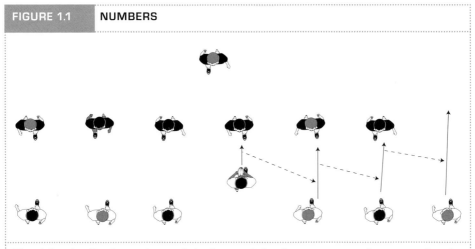

The defensive line is made up of six players defending seven attackers, creating the overlap.

Essential attack: Evasion

One-on-one

The most basic form of attack is the one-on-one, and there is no better weapon in such a contest than the sidestep. Not only can a sidestep beat a defender, but it can also create opportunities for support players as it draws in other defenders who have to cover. While it is undoubtedly one of the most productive skills in the game, sidestepping is also one of the least coached. Many consider it to be an innate skill, but instead it should be viewed as a technical skill like any other that can and should be developed to a high standard.

The simplest version is one well-timed step that is used to beat a defender who is stretched and has to cover across field at pace. This is called a 'one-step', and is developed in the drills in Part Two (see pages 81–131).

A 'two-step' is more dynamic and can beat a defender who is lined up straight ahead. The two-step simply combines two sidesteps, one immediately following the other. The ball carrier's first step fakes the direction of attack and aims to get the defender to shift his balance to one side, then his next step drives him to the other side. So, to get around a defender on the left, the ball carrier steps first off his left foot and then off his right; to get around a defender on the right, he steps first off his right foot and then off his left. Players can make their two-step more dynamic by turning their head and hips on the first step to make the fake more

Fiji's Vili Satala steps inside and tests Hong Kong's inside cover.

believable. The step will also be more effective when performed at pace, though players like Fiji's Waisale Serevi prove that, with power and coordination, side-steps can beat defenders from a stationary position. Simple 10 m² grids should be set up to allow players to practise their one-steps and two-steps and experiment with combining steps to beat a player.

COMBINE STEPS TO BEAT STEADY DEFENDERS

Players should combine sidesteps and experiment with footwork patterns to develop their ability to beat a player. A one-step can beat a defender who is moving sideways at pace, but two- and three-step combinations need to be developed to upset the balance of defenders who are steady.

Two-on-one

Beyond the one-on-one, which relies on individual skill, the next most fundamental form of attack is the two-on-one. Sevens is a simple game, and certainly not about developing ploys to master a seven-on-seven situation; the game is far simpler than that. Because of the amount of space on the pitch, defenders can easily be isolated and targeted, such that a two-on-one can be created anywhere on the field with purposeful running and accurate running lines. It doesn't matter if there are seven in a defensive line or seventeen: two attackers running at one defender with intent and tenacity can create a half-break or a line-break which, with the right support play, can mean try time!

The timing of the pass in a two-on-one situation is important: pass too early and the defender can move out to cover the support runner; pass too late and the defender can block or intercept the pass. However, the most crucial thing about a two-on-one is that both players run at pace. Often, the ball carrier will slow down to time his pass, which just means that the defender stays balanced and has a better chance of covering both attackers. It also means the timing has to be absolutely perfect. Instead, the ball carrier must run hard and maintain his speed to engage and fix the defender. The support runner must then accelerate in to the space to get through and behind the defensive line as quickly as possible. The general rule is all outside passes in a two-on-one situation should be dead flat to give the defender no chance to cover the support player; inside passes should be slightly deeper to avoid interception. These rules are reversed if the defender approaches the ball carrier from the outside.

LOOK FOR TWO-ON-ONES

The simplest form of decision-making is a two-on-one situation. Basically, a two-on-one puts a player into space, which is what rugby is all about. Two-on-one situations exist everywhere on the field: it is up to the players to go looking for and find them. Attacking players need to be assertive and determined in the way they attack individual players.

A framework for attack: the link pattern

Sevens is a fantastic game to play but can be extremely physically demanding. Compared with the 15-a-side game, the ball is in play for relatively longer periods of time with fewer stoppages and fewer opportunities to recover. Teams should therefore aim to play with more efficiency. In sevens, this means adopting a more structured approach to the game. Rather than stifling flair, structure gives players a framework on the field. This allows them to express their skills with more assurance, knowing that there is a clear model to revert to when play becomes disorganised. Establishing a framework where players have clearly defined roles and responsibilities also makes the coach's job much simpler.

Structure and width can be achieved in a sevens team by playing the 'link' pattern. The link is a player who positions between two attacking units of three players, producing a 3–1–3 formation. The primary role of the link player is to facilitate width and movement of the ball within the team. To fulfil this responsibility he must maintain a deep and wide position. The link also sets the attacking alignment for the players outside him and ensures that they have sufficient time and space to move and make decisions.

Basically, while one unit attack on one side of the field, the other unit realign in preparation for their turn to attack. Players therefore do not have to cover the whole pitch in support; instead, they just need to focus on supporting the players in their attacking unit on their side of the field. The deep position of the link also provides an important option in support if the ball carrier chooses to recoil from contact and clear the ball from pressure. From a scrum or a lineout, the scrum half seamlessly fits into the link position, but as play develops and players interchange positions, every player must have a good understanding of the pattern and work effectively to maintain it (see figure 1.2).

DEPTH MEANS TIME ON THE BALL

A deep alignment gives the attack time to move the ball. This needs to be tempered with the fact that it also gives the defence more time to organise. However, there is not such a preoccupation with the gain line in 7s as there is in 15s, so players should feel comfortable going backwards in order to move the ball to a different area to go forwards.

There are three broad scenarios that need to be considered with the link pattern depending on which player in the team takes the ball into contact: the link player himself, the player alongside the link (1st receiver), or wider players (centre and wing). Support play will be looked at in more detail in later chapters, but the general rule is that the player on the inside and the player on the outside of the ball carrier form the attacking unit. This unit will sometimes include the link

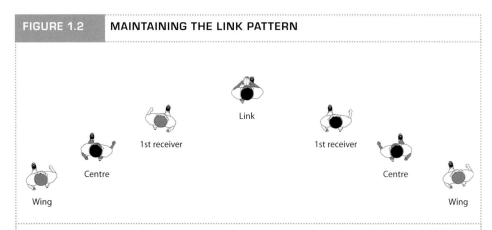

FIGURE 1.2   MAINTAINING THE LINK PATTERN

Link

1st receiver

1st receiver

Centre

Centre

Wing

Wing

Once a set piece is over, players interchange positions and use the terms above to communicate their role in an attacking situation quickly and clearly, for example 'I'm link' or 'I'm first' and so on. The coach can also use these terms in analysis to refer to a specific player in unbroken play.

player. When the link player is drawn into an attacking movement, the link position will need to be filled by another player in the team in order for the pattern to continue. This process of continuously regenerating the pattern after it has broken down, performed with speed and efficiency, is the key to the link system.

It is important to note that the link pattern is dependent on the ability of the attacking unit to win and clear the ball in tackle situations. The link player should never have to abandon his position to assist in contact, which would result in a damaging loss of width in the attacking team.

Scenario 1

The link pattern is most straightforward when the centre or wing takes the ball into contact, because the link will not be involved in the attacking unit and can therefore retain his position between the units in the middle of the pitch. As soon as the link player becomes the player two-in from the ball, that is when the player outside him passes the ball, he should quickly move into his deep position as shown in figure 1.3. The other unit will also not be disrupted if the centre or wing attacks and can valuably stay intact. When the pattern breaks down, the simplest way to regain structure and restore the pattern is to deliberately attack through the centre or wing channel.

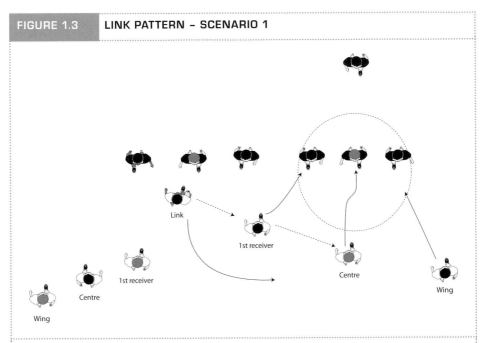

FIGURE 1.3   LINK PATTERN – SCENARIO 1

Link

1st receiver

Centre

Wing

1st receiver

Centre

Wing

When the centre or wing takes the ball into contact, the link player can conveniently retain his position in the middle of the pitch.

Scenario 2

It would be quite limiting to always attack using the centre and wing and impractical to expect one player to stay in the link position all the time. When the player outside the link initiates a move or makes a break, the link player has to surrender his position and commit to the attacking movement as an inside support player while the centre runs the outside support line. The player inside the link, which in this situation is the 1st receiver from the other unit, should fall back to become the new link for the team (see figure 1.4). This new link player gives the ball carrier an immediate option of passing back to relieve pressure. Alternatively, if a tackle is made he should scan the defence to decide whether to attack to the right side of the pitch with the wing as his support player, or back to the left towards his original attacking unit. The right wing must also assess the defence and decide whether it would be more worthwhile to stay out wide or move in to take over the link position, which would effectively re-establish a 3–1–3 formation.

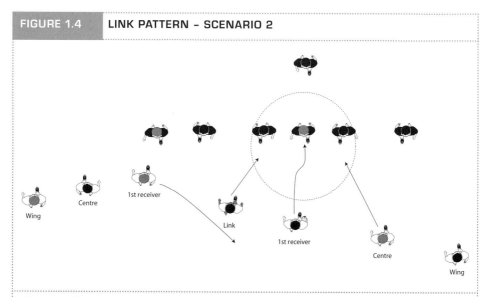

FIGURE 1.4   **LINK PATTERN – SCENARIO 2**

When the link player is drawn in to an attacking movement, another player must take up the role of link as quickly as possible. Here, this is the player inside the link and two-in from the ball.

Scenario 3

There are also times when the link player himself has the chance to make a break and, as illustrated in figure 1.5, the players on his inside and outside must move up to support him. This will obviously affect the attacking units on either side. As the pattern dictates, the player two-in from the ball should move quickly to assume the important role of link – in this case, that player is the centre. He should then actively assess the defence to decide which direction to attack, left or right. There may be a clear opportunity to attack back towards the right side of the field with his wing, but it may be a better option to attack left in such a situation because there will be two attackers in position to receive the ball. If the link decides to join them, he will restore the idea of an attacking unit of three and effectively restart the pattern.

| FIGURE 1.5 | LINK PATTERN – SCENARIO 3 |

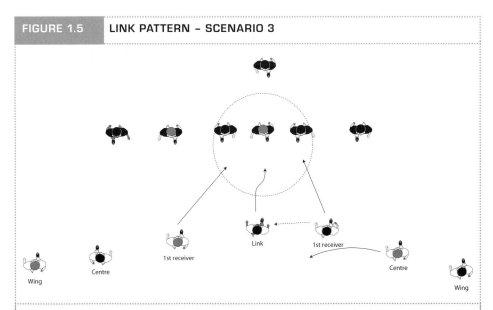

When the link takes the ball into contact, the player two-in from the ball takes up the link position and proceeds to direct the attack.

2 ATTACKING MOVEMENT PATTERNS

A GAME OF SUPPORT

The traditional concept of support in sevens involves players passing and then falling in behind the player to whom they have just passed so that they are in a position to receive the ball back immediately. This style of support play often creates a situation where the attack are successful in keeping possession but ultimately fail to penetrate the defence, as such a defensive style of support play exerts little pressure on the opposition. A better option is to have the player *two-in* from the ball carrier dropping back to a support position so that the players alongside the ball carrier can commit to the attacking movement. The support player who takes up this role is called a 'link', not only because he is an immediate and safe connection to wider positioned players, but also to fit in with the link pattern explained in Chapter 1 (see pages 7–11). This variation on tradition provides more direct and advantageous options for the attacking team and enables the use of set attacking movement patterns.

The attacking movement patterns on pages 14–24 are based on the idea of making defenders move to create space for the attack. They can be called and run spontaneously at any time because they involve only the players closest to the ball carrier – that is the player on his inside and the one on his outside. When the ball carrier successfully breaks through the defensive line, his two supporting teammates must be very quick to run past the defenders to support the break. This is called 'fast-breaking support' and should happen with every line-break. As a three-man attacking unit, these players must also work together to ensure that if the ball carrier is tackled to ground, there is a player near enough to protect the ball and another player to get the ball away.

FAST-BREAKING SUPPORT

Fast-breaking support in 7s is when attackers support the player who makes a break quickly and in numbers. Support players should be quick to follow the ball through the defensive line and give the ball carrier options to beat the sweeper. They should always be quicker to get to the ball carrier than the defence, who will have to turn and chase.

Attacking movement patterns

Stay-out

It is essential that attacking players know which defender is marking them at all times so that they know what options are available and where opportunities may arise. The first thing a ball carrier should do upon receiving the ball is scan the defence and quickly identify who is marking him. A 'stay-out' is used when the defenders are organised and in position opposite the attackers. The aim of the stay-out attacking movement pattern is to unsettle the defence by forcing them to move and make decisions.

IDENTIFY YOUR MARKER EARLY

It is very important in attack that players keep looking at the defence to see who is marking them. By analysing their marker's position and movement, they will be better able to make the correct decision to beat him.

FIGURE 2.1(A)	STAY-OUT – OPTION 1

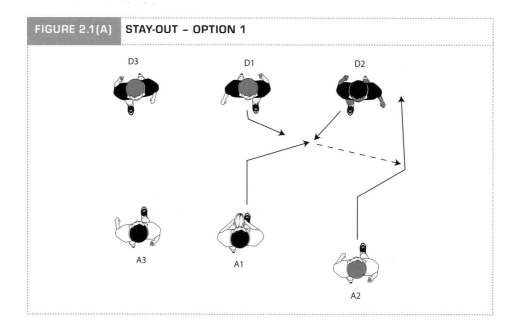

The ball carrier (A1) tries to engage and draw the defender who is marking the player outside him. He does this by initially running straight at the man opposite him, then changing direction sharply with a sidestep and accelerating towards the defender outside him. This puts pressure on the outside defender (D2) to decide whether to come in to tackle the ball carrier or stay out on the outside attacker. Whatever he does, the attack have a chance to break the line. If the defender decides to leave the man he is marking and come in for the ball carrier, the ball carrier plays a simple two-on-one where the outside attacker (A2) hits a flat, well-timed pass at pace (see figure 2.1(a)).

The attacking players outside the ball should initially mirror the angle of the ball carrier's run to draw their opponents out, creating more space for the ball carrier to attack. The outside defender (D2) *should* stay out on his man, so if the ball carrier is quicker than his opponent (D1), he will break through the line. The ball carrier should be single-minded in his attempt to draw the outside defender and back himself to beat his opposite man on the outside. However, if the defender (D1) is quick enough to cover him, his sliding movement will just as profitably create space on the inside that can be exploited with a switch (see figure 2.1(b)).

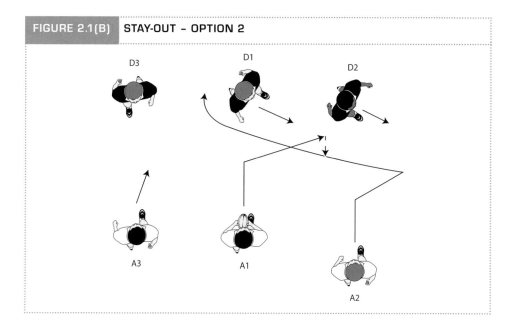

FIGURE 2.1(B) **STAY-OUT – OPTION 2**

The outside attacker (A2) should keep his eyes on the player marking the ball carrier (D1) and judge if and when he needs to change his angle to run the switch. As soon as the ball carrier steps and starts running across, A2 should turn his body dynamically towards the ball carrier to give the impression he is going to run a switch, then turn back sharply to stay outside. This action is called a 'shake'. The defenders will hold their positions in anticipation of a switch, giving the ball carrier a better chance to break through the line. If the ball carrier is still covered after the shake, the outside player then runs and calls for a late switch. The change of angle for a switch must always be dynamic and coincide with a change of pace to give the defence no chance to adjust. The player inside the ball carrier (A3) must also commit to the attack and run for an inside pass. This is especially useful if the outside attacker is too flat and does not have the angle to run a switch, or runs the switch too late.

England's David Strettle and Mathew Tait combine to stretch and beat the French defence.

Quick-switch

Since there is little room for innovation in sevens defence, it is relatively easy to predict how defenders are going to react to a situation. This knowledge can be used to manipulate and beat defences. To defend a switch, for example, the defender marking the ball carrier will usually stop following the ball, hold his position and shift his focus to covering the player running in to his channel. This defender effectively has to stop momentarily while he adjusts his focus and angle of run, and this is what is exploited in a 'Quick-switch'.

When a switch is executed very late and very close to the tackle-line, it is extremely difficult to defend because the defenders will be committed to their men and have no time to adjust. This is the kind of switch that may happen in a

'Stay-out' (see pages 14–16). In a 'Quick-switch', however, the ball carrier calls the movement early to allow the defence to see the switch happening. He runs quite a flat angle to give the outside support player as much time and space as possible to complete the movement pattern. It is important that, after making the switch pass, the attacker (A1) works hard to get into a wide and deep position as quickly as possible to support.

FIGURE 2.2	QUICK-SWITCH

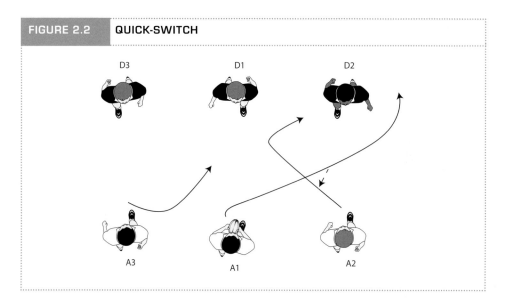

The outside support player (A2) should run an angle straight towards the defender who has held his channel (D1), to make the defender think he has covered the intended attack. A2 then sharply changes both his angle and pace to attack back out towards the original ball carrier (see figure 2.2). It effectively becomes a race between A2 and D1 to get to the space outside. The initiative is with the ball carrier (A2) since he knows he is going to change direction, while the defender (D1) has to wait for A2 to move and then react as quickly as possible to try to catch up. The attacker should also take the switch pass at speed to fix the defender, then consider the timing of his angle change. If the attacker steps too early, the defender will be able to cover him before he breaks through the line; if he steps too late, he will be tackled.

The ball carrier should then not only aim to get away from his defender, but should also try to draw the defender outside (D2) to create a two-on-one opportunity with the player who originally gave him the switch pass. If the defender (D1) does manage to cover the ball carrier, the attacker who initiated the move (A1) should run another switch, which this time will be late enough to beat the defence: the defender who has scrambled to cover the 'Quick-switch' will rarely be able to adjust his run to defend the second switch.

> ### SUPPORT PLAYERS MUST COMMIT TO LINES OF RUNNING
>
> It is vital that support players commit to their lines of running in order to pull defenders to create space. If they are running for an inside ball, they should run through even if they think there is no gap. Attackers need to play *through* the opposition defence, not in front of it.

As in all of the attacking movement patterns, the player inside the ball carrier should commit to the attack and provide an inside support option. In the 'Quick-switch', the inside attacker (A3) should time his run quite late for an inside pass off the ball carrier in order to avoid being covered by his defender (D3). He must also be prepared for the inside pass to be made before contact or during the tackle. His late run will also ensure he does not impede his team-mates if they run the second switch.

You-and-me

The 'You-and-me' is another attacking movement pattern that exploits established defensive systems. As discussed earlier, it is possible to be fairly accurate in predicting how defenders will move and react in most situations: as the attacking team move the ball the defence have to make sure they cover all players on the outside, so in effect the last defender covers the last attacker, the second last defender marks the second last attacker and so on. This is called 'numbering up' from the outside, and is the most common defensive pattern used to prevent the attack achieving an overlap out wide (see also pages 51–2). Furthermore, teams have to play with a sweeper in defence, which means there will always be a player on the attacking team left unmarked. This player is generally the last attacker on the opposite side of the field to where the ball is headed (see figure 2.3(a)). Suddenly changing the direction of attack towards the unmarked player can be a very effective way of achieving an overlap and beating the defence.

If the ball carrier simply stops and passes back to the side from which the ball came, the defence will have a chance to adjust and cover the overlap. In contrast, a 'You-and-me' is performed very close to the defenders, giving them little time to respond to the change of direction. It also misleads them about the intended area of attack and pulls them in one direction, creating space and an overlap on the other side of the field.

The ball carrier (A4) calls the 'You-and-me' with the man inside him (A3), then attacks the space outside his opposite man (D4). The 'You-and-me' call is a signal for the inside player to run a line for an inside pass, effectively at the same angle as the ball carrier. The covering defender (D3) will comfortably cover the inside

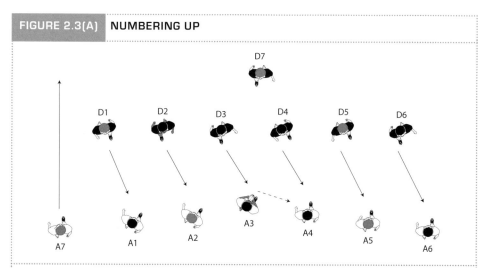

FIGURE 2.3(A) NUMBERING UP

As the attack move the ball towards the right-hand side of the field, the player on the far left (A7) will be left unmarked.

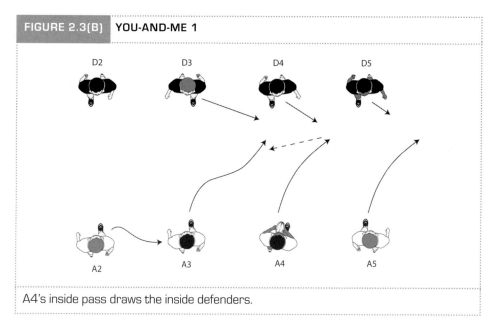

FIGURE 2.3(B) YOU-AND-ME 1

A4's inside pass draws the inside defenders.

run, and the defence will think they have detected the intended attack (see figure 2.3(b)). However, immediately after giving the inside pass, A4 quickly runs around the inside runner (A3) and receives the ball back at once, executing what could be termed an 'inside loop'. The covering defender (D3) has to move across to close the

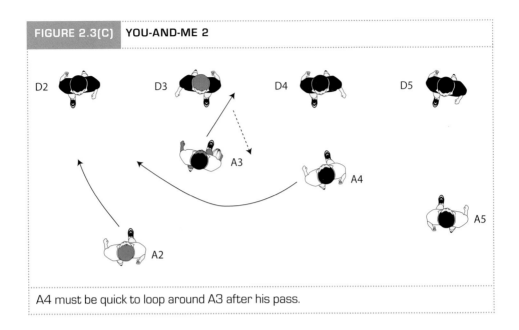

FIGURE 2.3(C)   YOU-AND-ME 2

D2   D3   D4   D5

A3

A4

A5

A2

A4 must be quick to loop around A3 after his pass.

gap for the inside runner, which forces the whole defensive line to slide across to cover with him. This pulls the defence and creates the overlap (see figure 2.3(c)). When the attacker receives the ball back on his looping run, he must quickly scan the defence to identify where the space is. If the inside defenders fail to slide across, there will be an opportunity for the ball carrier to run and break through the defensive line immediately. If the whole defensive line slides to cover the inside pass, as they should do, space will be created further out, and the ball carrier should quickly move the ball out wide to exploit the overlap.

Run-round-me

Attack in sevens is all about movement. Players should understand that where an attacking player moves, the defender marking him tends to move too. This idea can then be manipulated to beat defences.

A 'loop' in rugby terms is when an attacking player passes the ball and then runs around the receiver. The way the defence adjust to cover this movement can be predicted. As soon as he sees the passer loop, defender D1 will slide out to cover the receiver (A2), and the defender originally marking the receiver (D2) will then slide out to cover A1 on the loop (see figure 2.4(a)). If the looping player is quick, the defenders will also have to move at pace, and players moving sideways at speed are vulnerable to sidesteps and inside passes. This is exploited in a 'Run-round-me'.

While the movement in a 'Run-round-me' is effectively just a loop, it differs

FIGURE 2.4(A) LOOP

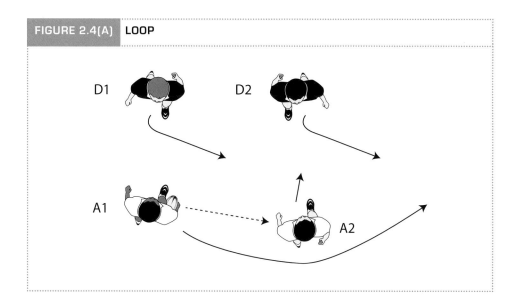

FIGURE 2.4(B) RUN-ROUND-ME

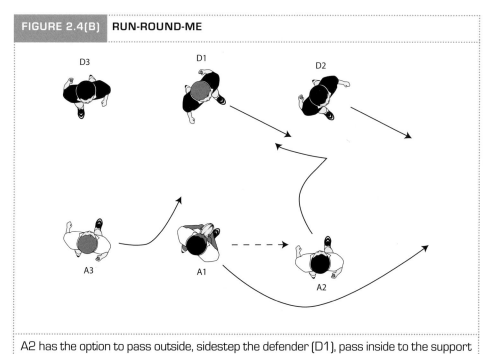

A2 has the option to pass outside, sidestep the defender (D1), pass inside to the support runner (A3) or dummy the inside pass and run around the support runner into space.

slightly from the loops typically coached in the 15-a-side game, where the attackers try to fix the defenders and beat them into the space before they have time to slide. In a 'Run-round-me', the attack *want* the defence to slide across and cover the looping player because opportunities will then open up on the inside. The ball carrier must be constantly watching how the defenders move because his actions will be determined by their reactions to the loop. Obviously, if the defenders decide not to slide to cover the looping player, there will be a clear overlap for the attackers on the outside.

As the defenders slide to cover the loop, the player with the ball (A2) has a number of options available to him and must make a decision based on the speed and angle of the defender D2's approach. If the defender is slow, the ball carrier may be able to beat him on the outside. Most often, however, the defender will move quickly to cover, which prevents an outside break but presents the ball carrier with a simple option of sidestepping him and breaking to the inside (see figure 2.4(b)).

The player originally inside the looping player (A3) should also commit to the attack and run for an inside pass off the ball carrier. Therefore, if the ball carrier is not confident of beating the defender with a sidestep, he can make an inside pass to A3; this also achieves the intention of beating the defence on the inside. The ball carrier should look to see if A3 is covered by the inside defender (D3), and if so he should consider dummying the pass to the inside runner and running around him into the space. Against good defences, the ball carrier should also consider playing a 'You-and-me' (see pages 18–20) with the inside runner, which in most cases will guarantee an overlap on the other side of the pitch.

Put-away

A 'Put-away' is another variation on a loop, but the timing of the looping player's movement is more delayed than in a 'Run-round-me' (see pages 20–22). Where the 'Run-round-me' invites the opposition to read the loop, the 'Put-away' aims to take the defence by surprise. Like many of the attacking movement patterns in this chapter, the 'Put-away' already exists in the game and players can often be seen running it off the cuff. These movement patterns beat defences even when they are run spontaneously, so when they are practised and then run with intent and purpose, players' coordination and timing is so much better.

The 'Put-away' works on the idea of playing behind the defence. Nowadays, defences are very well organised when the ball is in front of them, so getting in behind the defensive line often reaps high rewards: a line-break or half-break followed by an offload to a support player hitting the ball at pace never fails to devastate a defence. The 'Put-away' is effectively just an offload in the tackle, but one that is planned. Most offloads happen in a game on impulse when the ball

2 ATTACKING MOVEMENT PATTERNS

carrier gets his arms free in a tackle and a support player is running into space; the 'Put-away' *ensures* that both of these things happen.

Basically, the ball carrier aims to step inside the defender marking him, engage him in a tackle and make an immediate offload to a support runner outside (see figure 2.5). To make all this happen, the ball carrier must first identify which defender is marking him and then let the inside player know his intention: 'Hey, John, I'm going to put you away'. The ball carrier is not necessarily looking to beat the defender outright, just to get to his inside and stretch him enough so that the tackle is weak.

The ball carrier can use a two-step sidestep (see page 5) to get to the defender's inside. Another effective technique when the defender is lined up straight ahead is to 'bounce' to the inside. The 'bounce' involves jumping on to both feet towards the outside shoulder of the defender, making him momentarily flat-footed. As both feet land, the ball carrier springs off the outside foot to the inside of the defender and accelerates through the tackle. The success of the offload will be determined by the quality of the run, so the ball carrier must be dynamic in the way he moves. He should also maintain leg drive during contact and aim to keep the ball in two hands to make the offload.

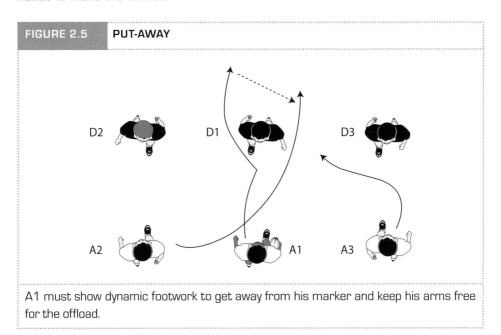

FIGURE 2.5	PUT-AWAY

A1 must show dynamic footwork to get away from his marker and keep his arms free for the offload.

The timing between the ball carrier and the inside support player (A2) is absolutely critical because a 'Put-away' is played through the tackle, so there is always a risk of losing the ball in contact. The offload has to be made almost immediately after contact, so if the support player runs too late the move will break down, and if he runs too early the defence will move to cover him. The support player *must* wait until the ball carrier steps inside the defender, then race to the outside to take the offload. It is also important that the support player runs a line as close to the tackler as possible to avoid being covered by other defenders.

The outside support player (A3) also plays a role in preserving the space targeted for attack. As soon as the play is called, he should stay wide but move up flat with the ball carrier. He should also call for the ball to draw the attention of his opponent (D3), deterring him from moving in to cover the offload to A2. This will also put him nearer to the tackle-line as a support player in case the move breaks down.

THE MAN OUTSIDE YOU IS RESPONSIBLE FOR YOUR ALIGNMENT

Outside attacking players should communicate to the player inside about maintaining depth in their alignment. Alignment is something that should be considered and deliberate, not just a case of players finding themselves in a position. Outside players can improve their chances of getting the ball if they force inside players to stay deep.

3 CONTINUITY
A GAME OF SUPPORT

When coaching the principle of continuity in sevens, more emphasis should be placed on support play *before* contact than on support *in* contact. Support players must work hard off the ball to give the ball carrier options to pass or offload out of the tackle. Every tackle situation presents an opportunity for the defenders to contest possession, and also gives them a chance to consolidate and reset their defensive line. The attacking team should therefore aim to keep the ball moving and avoid contact if possible, which will make it more difficult for the defence to stay organised.

However, there are times when taking contact is the best option, especially when there is a need to regain structure and depth in the attack. This could be when patterns have broken down or the defence are right up in the faces of the attackers, blocking the passing lanes. In these situations the ball carrier should seek contact to create offside lines, which importantly forces the opposition to retreat. The attackers must then aim to recycle the ball as quickly as possible before the defence have time to position and reorganise.

> **DO SOMETHING!**
> All players on the attacking team should always be active and looking to contribute. If he is not supporting the ball carrier in attack, he should be positioning himself for the next attack.

Due to the small number of players involved in sevens, the tackle area is relatively straightforward and does not need to occupy a large part of the training programme; technique in contact must be sound, but in most cases the priority should be getting a support player to the tackled player before a defender. Continuity is therefore more about speed of support than anything else, and it all starts way before any contact is made at all.

Avoiding contact: 'Easy'

There is no problem with running the ball into contact as long as the attackers are confident in their ability to secure possession in the tackle contest. The ball carrier's decision about whether or not to take contact must be based on his assessment of the situation and the state of the defence. If the defence are widely spread, the ball carrier may back himself or his support players to break the tackle or at least to offload the ball in contact to keep the ball alive. However, if the defence are compressed, there is a good chance that it will be more difficult to recycle the ball quickly in the tackle. In this situation, the ball carrier may decide that the best option is to avoid contact.

David Moonlight of Canada pulls back from the tackle to keep the ball out of contact.

The ball carrier must first be dynamic to stop forward momentum and recoil from contact, and then be quick to clear the ball from pressure. The ball carrier needs not only active support players on either side of him when attacking the defence, but also a support player in a deeper position for when he chooses to avoid contact. This is the link player explained in Chapter 1; that is, the player *two-in* from the ball carrier (see pages 7–11).

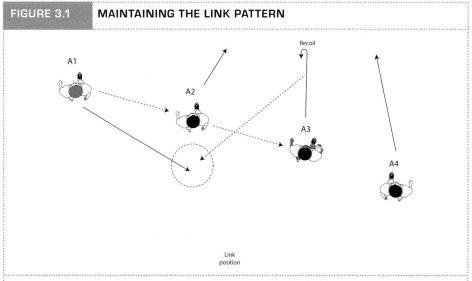

| FIGURE 3.1 | MAINTAINING THE LINK PATTERN |

A1 passes to A2 and supports. After A2 passes the ball, A1 is the player two-in from the ball and so moves into a deep position inside the ball to become the link player.

The link player can also initiate this action by calling 'Easy'. This is a signal for the ball carrier to pull out of an attacking movement and pass the ball back to the link immediately. The link player must show discipline and accurate judgement in making the 'Easy' call and not exploit it as a selfish means to get his hands on the ball. The call should only be made when strictly necessary, that is in the interests of continuity when the ball carrier could be in danger of losing possession if he continued on his line of run. The link player can also make the 'Easy' call if, in his assessment of the situation and the state of the defence, there is a better opportunity elsewhere on the

THE MAN WHO TAKES THE BALL IN IS RESPONSIBLE FOR GETTING IT OUT

The ball carrier should be made responsible for ensuring that the ball is recycled effectively. If he knows that he will be made accountable if the ball is lost, he will work harder to protect the ball as soon as contact is made, which is the most critical time in terms of success in contact. Players tend to rely too much on support in contact situations.

field; however, he must only make the call if there are players in a good position outside him to take advantage of it.

Players have to understand that it is not good practice to keep pulling back in attack, as it gives the defence a chance to move up and apply increasing pressure. The attacking team must avoid making successive 'Easy' calls for this reason, but also because it flattens out the attacking alignment and results in a damaging loss of depth in their support play. Players should therefore be encouraged to back themselves, commit to the attacking movement patterns as much as possible and be confident about taking contact.

Managing contact: 'Hold' or 'Clear'

It is worth repeating that in sevens the success of a contact situation is most often determined by what is done *before* contact, not *during* contact. Since the attacking movement patterns involve three players, contact should be managed by the same three players and ideally no more. If a fourth player has to move in to help secure possession, the attacking team will lose width and options and the initiative will shift to the defending team. Each player who is involved in the attacking movement pattern also has an important role to play when contact is made: the ball carrier should be made chiefly responsible for retaining the ball in contact, and the two supporting players should then combine to efficiently secure and clear the ball away from pressure.

SUPPORT IN THREES

It must be drummed in to players that three players are needed at every tackle situation: the ball carrier, a player to secure possession and a player to clear the ball from pressure. Even if this is not always the case, players must treat it as a rule that the ball carrier needs two supporting players.

The ball carrier

When the ball carrier cannot avoid contact, it is important that he is tackled on his own terms. This means that, wherever possible, he should run into the space between defenders and try to evade the tackle with dynamic footwork and fend. If the ball carrier runs straight into a defender, the defender will have the time and position to set up for an offensive, front-on tackle. Instead, the ball carrier should use steps to make the defender move just before contact, which invariably results in a softer, side-on tackle. This kind of contact enables the ball carrier to either offload in the tackle or present the ball with more control to his support players.

New Zealand support players are quick to react and support their team mate, Onosa Tololima-Auva'a, as he strikes at Argentina's defence.

Support players

The actions of the primary support player are dictated first by what is happening in front of him and second by what he is being told from behind. His main aim should be to try to run in to space and take an offload to keep the ball alive. However, if the ball carrier is smothered and unable to release the ball, the primary support player should go in to rip and free the ball. If the ball carrier is tackled to ground, the primary support player has two options: to *hold* over the ball or to *clear* beyond the ball. His action is determined by the secondary support player, who calls 'hold' or 'clear' depending on his proximity to the ruck: if he is very close to the ruck, he should call 'clear' to instruct the primary support player to clean out the defender; if he is still quite a distance from the ruck, he should call for the primary support player to 'hold' over the ball to buy time for him to get there and play the ball. This concept of the secondary support player dictating action results in better management of the tackle area and, importantly, forces the players to always work in threes.

The support players should aim to anticipate when contact is going to occur and move to secure possession instantaneously. The idea of *synchronised* attacking play reflects the speed at which players should be expected to respond to a tackle. There is a notable difference in terms of speed and success in continuity between support players who anticipate and those who watch and then react. 'Ball-watching' is a term used when players spectate instead of participate and it is one of the most common causes of poor support play. Players must develop the ability to assess situations as they happen on the pitch by judging both the movements of the ball carrier and the state of the defence. They should then predict what is going to happen and act on it. To develop this quality in the players, the coach has to focus on the players *off* the ball and assess their contribution.

> **TAKE THE TACKLER TO GROUND**
> The ball carrier should be conscious never to go to ground before the tackler. If the defender manages to stay on his feet in the tackle, he will be in an immediate position to steal the ball on the ground. The ball carrier should therefore maintain leg drive in contact, which more often than not will force the tackler to go to ground to complete the tackle.

Technique in contact

The ball carrier

The ball carrier should always aim to stay on his feet in contact and look for a support player to keep the ball alive. If he is unable to offload the ball immediately, he should still avoid going to ground to set up a ruck. Instead, he should turn aggressively towards his team, sink at the knees to lower his centre of gravity and widen his base of support. He should also be dynamic, using shoulder rolls and elbows to break the tackler's grip and quickly pop the ball back to a close support player to clear the ball from pressure.

When contact with the ground is unavoidable or desired, the ball carrier can call on two techniques: a 'tunnel-ball' or a 'long place'.

Tunnel-ball

The tunnel-ball is the practice of hitting the ground on the forearms and knees and pushing the ball back through the legs. This is an effective way of concealing and protecting the ball from the opposition and also buys time for support players. However, there are some safety concerns with this technique, and players should therefore be coached to keep their chin off their chest and look forwards at all times when performing a tunnel-ball. Another concern with this technique is that it generally requires the ball carrier to stay square with the tackler when contact is made, which not only contradicts the idea of attacking space but also makes it easier for the defender to prevent an offload. There is also the possibility that the tackled player will be penalised by the referee for deliberately lying over the ball and not rolling away. This technique should notably be avoided with junior and youth players.

Long place
The safer method of ball presentation is a long place. This is similar to a conventional placement, but instead of hitting the ground with a straight body parallel to the try line and placing the ball at arms' length, the tackled player uses his abdominal muscles to place the ball much further back. The body should form into a 'V' shape as the player places the ball as far back as possible towards his own team, aiming for a spot and in line with his feet (see figure 3.2).

FIGURE 3.2	BODY POSITION FOR A LONG PLACE

This technique makes it more difficult for the opposition to reach over and get their hands on the ball than in a conventional placement. Notably, the long place also allows the ball carrier to evade defenders and attack space because the momentum in a side-tackle can be used to fall into the correct body position.

Support players
The primary support player will be required to either bridge over the ball ('hold') or clean out beyond the ball ('clear') in a tackle situation.

'Hold' (bridging)
Bridging demands considerable control in order that the ball is not exposed at the back of the ruck. The primary support player should adopt a low body position with his head up, looking forwards, and establish a wide base of support with his feet. It is important that the player keeps his chin off his chest and is self-supporting with his shoulders above his hips. Bridging is an easy concept, but it takes practice to approach a tackle area at speed but also with sufficient balance and control to hold over the tackled player and ball.

ALWAYS ANTICIPATE IN SUPPORT
Players need to be constantly reading and anticipating play. If they do, they will be far quicker to support the ball carrier to a break, keep the ball alive or recycle possession in a tackle. Players shouldn't watch the ball – they should assess the situation between the ball carrier and the defence and then react accordingly.

'Clear'

The technique of clearing rucks is more familiar to players than bridging. In this situation, the primary support player should approach from directly behind the ball in a low body position and target the limbs of the players attacking possession. If a defender is reaching over with his hands on the ball, the first support player should match his body height, hit with his shoulder and aim to get an arm under the opponent's arm. This is called a 'Punch-arm' and valuably serves to both lower the attacker's body height and prevent the defender from picking up the ball. If the defender has stepped over the ball, the primary support player should lift the opponent's front leg and drive him backwards. Fundamentally, on a 'clear' call the primary support player should aim to hit the tackle area with speed and aggression and maintain leg drive throughout contact.

KEEP THE BALL MOVING

Every time the ball is stationary, the defence have an opportunity to organise. The attack should therefore aim to always keep the ball moving. To achieve this, support players must work hard off the ball to give the ball carrier an option to pass, especially in contact where players should pass out of the tackle wherever possible. An active ball presents a constant problem for the defence.

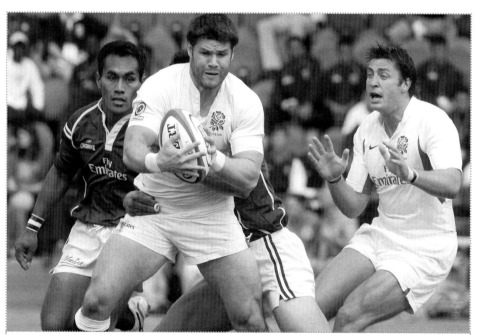

Rob Thirlby of England is quick and vocal in support of Danny Hipkiss, giving him an option to offload the ball out of the tackle.

4 STARTER PLAYS AND SET PIECES
A GAME OF POSSESSION

Starter plays: strikes and playbacks

A starter play is a rehearsed movement pattern from a scrum or a lineout. A starter play can take the form of a *strike*, which is an immediate attempt to break the defensive line, or a *playback*, which aims to pull the defenders to one side of the field before attacking on the other side.

When the attack intend to strike, their aim is to put the defence under pressure quickly. Most of the attacking movement patterns in Chapter 2 (see pages 13–24) are ideal for starter play strikes, but slightly more complicated patterns can also be used from a set piece because there is more time to plan and communicate.

Playbacks are special plays from scrums and lineouts that aim to stretch the defence to breaking point. The attacking team effectively fake an attack on one side of the field to create an overlap on the other side of the field. The key to a playback is that, once the attack have pulled the defence across, the change in direction coincides with a sudden change in pace. This should be played like the 'Numbers' call in unbroken play (see pages 3–4), where the aim is to get the ball into the space before the defenders have time to cover. Players should generally aim to avoid contact in a playback, but should also be careful not to align too deeply as this will allow the defence time and space to apply pressure and cover the overlap. Playbacks can be performed by going in to contact as a way to fully commit defenders, but the attackers must be totally confident in their ability to recycle the ball quickly in the tackle.

The choice of starter play is determined both by the situation and by how the defenders are expected to react in that situation. All things being equal, the following starter plays will work well from the suggested scenarios, but it is worth keeping an open mind about their use from set pieces in other areas of the field. For example, a move suggested for a right-field scrum *can* work from a left-field scrum, scrum plays *can* work from lineouts and so on. It all depends on how the defence react; this is something that can be predicted, but more importantly must be analysed by the players themselves during a game. It is important to emphasise to players that patterns and plays should not replace decision-making, but simply put forward ideas and options to help simplify the decision-making process.

Right-field scrum
Strike 1

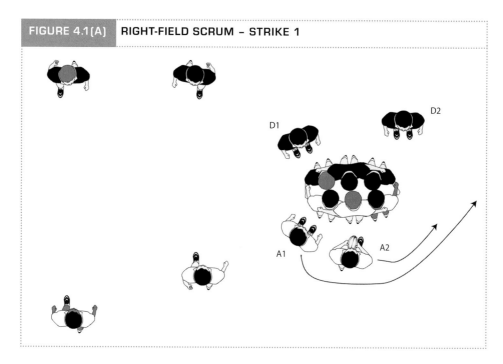

FIGURE 4.1(A) RIGHT-FIELD SCRUM – STRIKE 1

The players start off as shown in figure 4.1(a) with the fly half (A2) standing directly behind the hooker in the scrum. The scrum half (A1) puts the ball into the scrum and immediately loops around the fly half, who is standing directly behind the hooker. The fly half picks up the ball and runs quickly to draw defender D2 for a two-on-one with the scrum half on the outside. The attacking hooker should break right in this situation to provide a deep option in support of the ball carrier (see figure 4.1(a)). The fly half can also consider a grubber kick through the defence since the opposing scrum half (D1) will not be in a sweeping position.

Strike 2

This starter play is effectively a planned 'Run-round-me' (see pages 20–22) on the wing. The fly half (A1) throws a miss pass to the wing (A3), with the centre (A2) looping early and at pace. The speed of the centre's looping run is essential to stretch the defence, so it is not a bad idea to use your quickest player in this

| FIGURE 4.1(B) | RIGHT-FIELD SCRUM – STRIKE 2 |

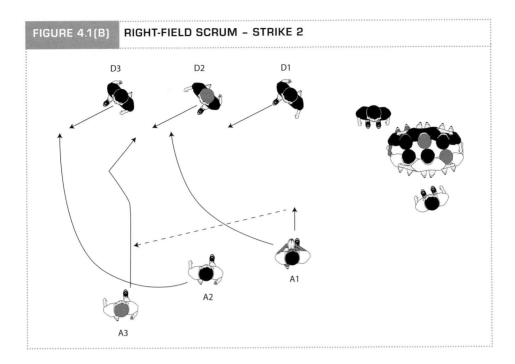

position for the starter move. The fly half follows his pass and runs an inside line off the ball carrier. The wing should initially run straight, then head out as if looking to use the looping player. As the defenders stretch to cover, the winger should step in to isolate the opposition centre (D2) and either pass to the fly half running the inside line or run around him and the man marking him (D1) into space (see figure 4.1(b)).

An effective variation on this play is a 'Run-round-me' on the centre. The fly half passes to the centre and loops around him, and the scrum half runs for the inside pass off the centre. The loop creates a gap between the defending fly half and his forwards, especially if the defending hooker breaks left from the scrum to cover the short side.

Strike 3

This is a double switch (see pages 17–18). The fly half (A2) receives the ball from the scrum half (A1) and immediately passes to the centre (A3). The centre initially runs forwards, then runs across field to perform a switch with the wing (A4). The wing must time his run quite late and move quickly to engage the opposition and fix the opposition centre (D3) in his position. The wing then switches again with the fly half (see figure 4.1(c)). The timing and pace of the fly half's run onto the second switch is the key to ensuring that the defence are beaten by the movement.

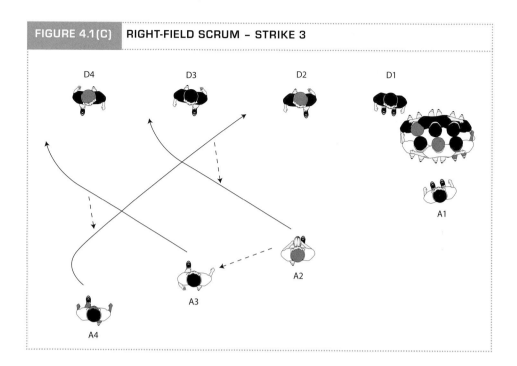

FIGURE 4.1(C) RIGHT-FIELD SCRUM – STRIKE 3

A two-on-one situation is created with the fly half and centre attacking the opposition wing (D4).

Left-field scrum
Strike 1

This should be run in the same way as a 'Stay-out' attacking movement pattern (see pages 14–16), with the scrum half (A1) running at the defending fly half (D2) to draw him. The scrum half should be confident of beating the opposition hooker (D5) to the space inside the defending fly half. If he achieves this, the defending fly half has to come in to cover him, leaving a gap for the attacking team's fly half (A2) to run into (see figure 4.2(a)). If the defending hooker is quick and able to cover the scrum half's run, the attacking fly half should switch as directed by the 'Stay-out' pattern. The attacking hooker should also be quick to break from the scrum to support the scrum half on his inside, and the props should play their part by delaying their opponents' exit from the scrum.

Strike 2

This is effectively a 'Put-away' (see pages 22–24) and begins with a long fast miss pass from the fly half (A1) to the wing (A3). The wing runs hard at his opposite man (D3) to fix him. It is important that the attacking centre (A2) holds his

FIGURE 4.2(A)   LEFT-FIELD SCRUM – STRIKE 1

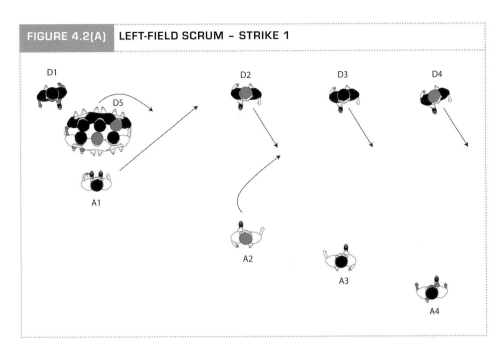

FIGURE 4.2(B)   LEFT-FIELD SCRUM – STRIKE 2

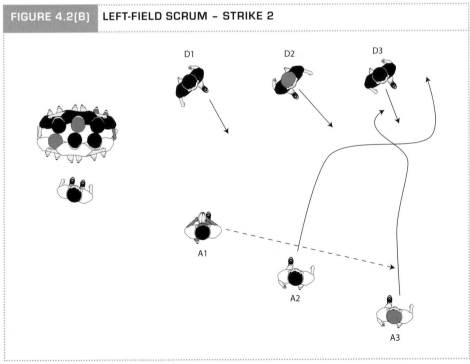

position and stays inside the wing to deter the opposition from sliding out. The wing steps sharply inside the defending wing (D3) and aims to keep his arms free in the tackle. The centre simultaneously runs to the wing's outside to take the offload (see figure 4.2(b)). The centre has the advantage over his opposite man (D2) because his acceleration to the outside is sudden and will catch the defending centre by surprise. The timing and coordination of the wing and the centre are the keys to success in this starter play.

Strike 3

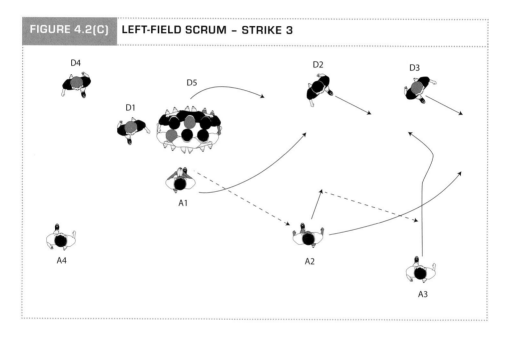

FIGURE 4.2(C) | **LEFT-FIELD SCRUM – STRIKE 3**

This starter play is another variation of the 'Run-round-me' attacking movement pattern (see pages 20–22). The backs adopt a split formation, with the wing (A2) and the centre (A3) on the right of the scrum and the fly half (A4) alone on the short side. The scrum half (A1) passes to the wing and follows his pass. The wing passes to the centre and loops around him as fast as possible to force the defenders to slide across at pace. The defending hooker (D5) will have to move a long way to cover the attacking scrum half, who runs an inside line off the centre (see figure 4.2(c)). The centre should fake a pass out to the looping player, then play a 'You-and-me' (see pages 18–20) with the scrum half. The scrum half must hit the ball at pace and may break the line without the need to pass back for the 'You-and-me'.

38

Centre-field scrum
Strike

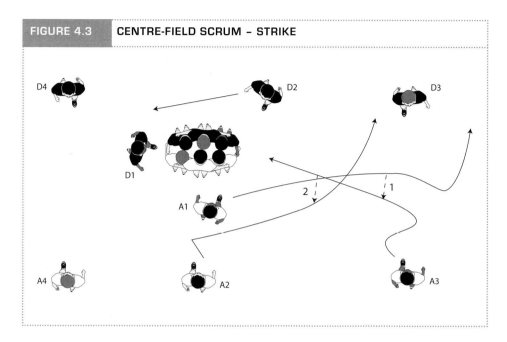

| FIGURE 4.3 | CENTRE-FIELD SCRUM – STRIKE |

This split formation from a centre-field scrum (see figure 4.3) allows for a variety of options. A double switch to the right is one option: as the ball is put into the scrum, the fly half (A2) runs left and calls for the ball as a decoy. This draws his opposite number (D2) across and creates space for the scrum half (A1) to run right. The scrum half picks up from the scrum and runs the first switch with the centre (A3). The centre then runs a second switch with the fly half, creating a two-on-one opportunity with the fly half and scrum half against the isolated defender (D3). The fly half should time his run so that he runs on to the second switch at full pace. The attacking hooker (A4) should break quickly from the scrum and run an inside line off the fly half.

Many of the starter plays suggested for scrums in other areas are also suitable for a scrum in centre-field. It is also worth noting that defenders are vulnerable to kicks from a centre-field scrum as they will be significantly isolated from support.

Lineout
Strike
This is a 'Quick-switch' (see pages 16–18) between the centre (A2) and the wing (A3), with the fly half (A1) looping around as fast as possible to the outside. The

| FIGURE 4.4 | LINEOUT – STRIKE |

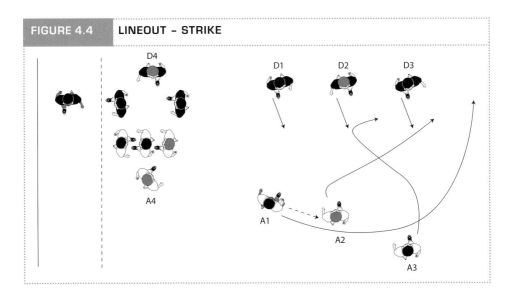

fly half must pass the ball to the centre as early as possible to allow time for the 'Quick-switch'. The wing should initially run an angle towards the defending centre (D2) to make the defenders feel confident they have the attackers covered, then change direction sharply to link up with the centre and the fly half. The scrum half (A4) should move into a deep position inside the ball carrier (see figure 4.4). If the defenders cover well, the centre can consider running another switch with the wing, but only as a decoy to hold up the defence; this creates a two-on-one with the attacking wing and fly half against the defending wing (D3). A long diagonal grubber kick by the centre is also an option, as the defending scrum half (D4) will have a long way to run to get into a sweeping position from a lineout.

Playback 1

This playback is a mixture of a 'Run-round-me' and a 'You-and-me' (see pages 20–22 and 18–20 respectively), and creates a big overlap back towards where the lineout first took place. The move begins with the scrum half (A1) passing to the fly half (A2), then following his pass to run an inside line off the centre (A3). The fly half then passes to the centre and loops around him at pace. The centre fakes interest in the looping player to make the defence slide and to draw the defending fly half (D2) across (see figure 4.5(a)). He then runs a 'You-and-me' with the scrum half and loops around him to link up with the forwards. As soon as the lineout is over, the forwards should quickly drop back in to an attacking alignment so that they are able to run on to the ball at pace when the ball comes back their way.

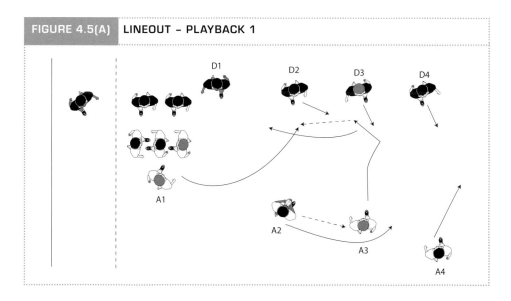

FIGURE 4.5(A) **LINEOUT – PLAYBACK 1**

Playback 2

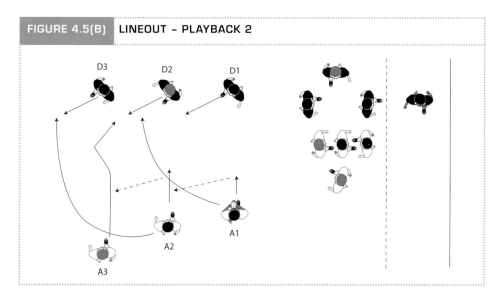

FIGURE 4.5(B) **LINEOUT – PLAYBACK 2**

This playback is very similar to one of the strike plays for a right-field scrum (see pages 34–35). In effect, it is a 'Run-round-me' movement pattern (see pages 20–22). The ball is passed out swiftly to the wing (A3). The centre (A2) loops as quickly as possible after his pass, which will force the defence to slide across the field to cover. The attacking fly half (A1) runs an inside line off the wing to draw the defending fly half (D1) across. The wing must first look outside to give the impression he is going to use the looping player, then step in and fake an inside pass to the fly half, who runs a decoy line through the defence. The wing then runs around the fly half's run to link up with the scrum half in the middle of the field and the forwards out wide on the other side (see figure 4.5(b)).

New Zealand's Orene Ai'I mixes pace and footwork to penetrate the French defence.

Set pieces

Lineout

Though there are few lineouts in sevens, they must still be practised to make sure a team never loses the ball on its own throw. In the options below, the player who throws the ball in to the lineout is also the player who receives it back from the jumper to pass out to the backs. The scrum half is usually chosen to throw the ball in, since he will be the player with the best clearing pass. The lineout does not need to be very complicated; if the defence are not competing for the ball in the air, a very basic option will often be enough to secure possession.

Option 1

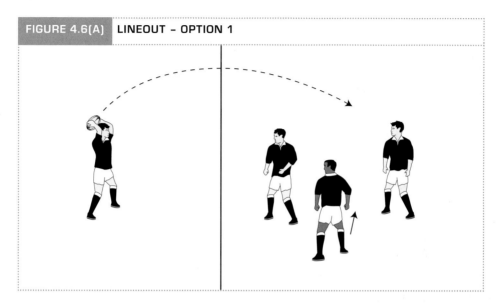

FIGURE 4.6(A)   **LINEOUT – OPTION 1**

In option 1, two forwards line up in the lineout, with the designated jumper just out of the lineout in the scrum half position. The jumper then enters the lineout between his two support players, who assist him in his jump for the ball (see figure 4.6(a)).

This basic set-up remains consistent for all lineouts, but if the defending players look poised to jump, the attacking team need to use movement to beat them. It is therefore necessary to observe how the opposition are setting up before making a call.

Option 2

In Option 2, the jumper enters the lineout very close to the back support player to tempt the opposition backwards. He then quickly runs forwards, followed by the back lifter, for a jump at the front (see figure 4.6(b)). The jumper should aim to jump forwards to make sure he gets his hands in front of those of his opponent.

Option 3

The success of any lineout largely depends on the quality of the throw in terms of its timing, weight and accuracy, so the number of options available at lineout time is determined by the competence of the thrower. Option 3 requires a lob-like throw from the scrum half, ensuring that the ball clears the opposition jumper. Here, the jumper and support team shuffle backwards to try to lose their markers (see figure 4.6(c)).

FIGURE 4.6(B) LINEOUT – OPTION 2

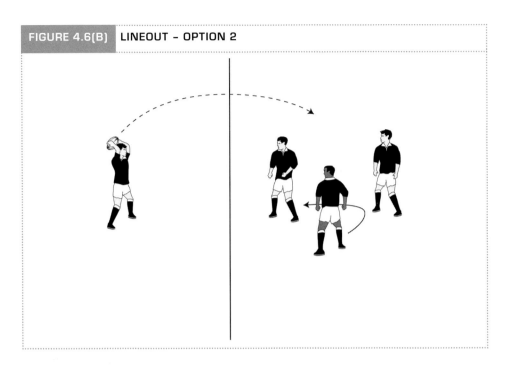

FIGURE 4.6(C) LINEOUT – OPTION 3

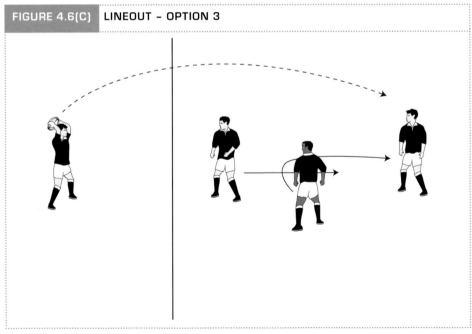

Option 4

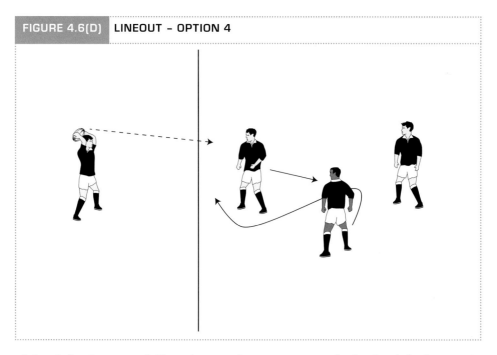

LINEOUT – OPTION 4

If the defending unit follow the attacking jumper to the back of the lineout, a fourth option can be considered. Again, the set-up is the same and the players move as if they were playing option 1 or 2, which makes it more difficult for the opposition to read the play. In option 4, the jumper dashes from between his support players to jump unsupported at the front of the lineout. The ball is thrown in quickly and tapped straight back to the scrum half, who then passes out to the backs (see figure 4.6(d)). The jumper's movement must be dynamic to beat the defence and the throw must be low and hard. It is important that the jumper allows the throw to cross the 5 m line to avoid giving away a free kick.

Option 5

The ball is usually given back to the scrum half off the top of the jump – that is, while the jumper is still in the air. This gets the attack under way quickly, but also allows the defence, particularly the defender at the back of the lineout, to start advancing just as quickly. For this reason, the scrum half should use a call to signal when he wants the jumper to land before giving him the ball. The defence then have to check their run and stay onside, which gives the scrum half more time to make a good pass and relieves the pressure on the attacking fly half.

FIGURE 4.6(E) | LINEOUT – OPTION 5

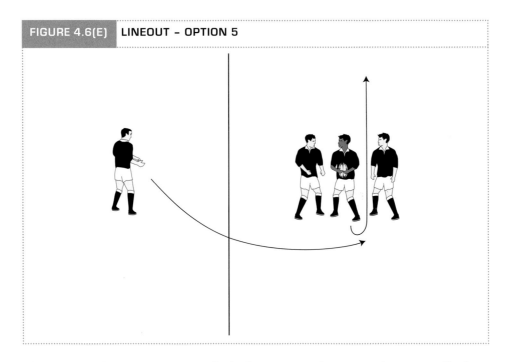

The action of landing to deliver the ball can be used as a set play, especially for a lineout close to the opposition try line. In option 5, the jumper lands with the ball and turns as usual towards his scrum half. Instead of giving the ball as expected to the scrum half, he fakes the pass, spins round and drives for the try line, powered by his support players (see figure 4.6(e)). In sevens, defenders rarely anticipate a drive from the lineout, so option 5 is a worthwhile and often try-scoring tactic close to the line; the worst that can happen is that the ball carrier will be tackled with two support players right alongside him.

Scrum

There are a few considerations at scrum time to ensure the team in possession retain the ball.

Binding

First, the players should consider how they bind on to one another. There are a couple of options: an *over-bind*, which is roughly the same way front row players bind in the 15-a-side game, where the hooker binds above the arms of the props; and an *under-bind*, where the hooker binds underneath the arms of the props, with the tops of his shoulders in the armpits of the props.

The advantage of the under-bind is that the hooker can get away from the scrum and enter the attack quickly. Modified laws have prohibited this option, but referees usually overlook this issue of binding. To put it into context, both Fiji and New Zealand used the under-bind without being penalised during the 2005 Rugby World Cup Sevens final. However, while the under-bind is certainly the preferred method, it positions the hooker a little further away from the ball and effectively leaves the two props to control and stabilise the scrum, which could cause problems against strong opposition.

In contrast, the advantage of the over-bind is that it makes for a more solid unit and therefore a more stable platform from which to release the ball. With this binding, the hooker will certainly be slower to leave the scrum, but this is no cause for concern as long as he is not part of the starter play. The best idea is to make players aware of both methods of binding and encourage them to consider the situation and the strengths of the opposition before choosing.

Whichever way the hooker decides to bind, the props should consistently aim to bind on each other and not on the hooker, facilitating a quicker release for the latter. This contradicts another guideline on binding, but it is another one that either goes unnoticed or is overlooked by referees. Furthermore, the props should try to delay their opponents leaving the scrum by holding them for a second or two after the ball is out. This leaves areas of the field undefended for a short time, which can be exploited in the starter plays.

Timing

The next major consideration at the scrum is the timing of the put-in. The best option is usually to give the opposition as little time as possible to disrupt the scrum, so the ball should be put in as soon as the scrum engages. To execute this, the players should squat quite low before engagement and drive upwards into their opposite man. This should be performed explosively and be coordinated so that the ball is in, out and away from the scrum very quickly.

However, if a team adopt this tactic at every scrum, the opposition will prepare for it. Variety in the timing of the put-in will make it more difficult for the opposition to anticipate the delivery of the ball. A deferred put-in is performed on a signal after engagement when the two front rows are settled. There is a good deal of strength required in this situation, so timing the put-in with a coordinated drive is essential. Verbal signals work very well to ensure that all members of the attacking front row drive at the same time. An American football call is suitable, where the scrum half calls 'hut-one-hut-two-hut-three' and the ball is delivered on a pre-determined 'hut'.

The base of the scrum

The base of the scrum tends to be a very untidy area of the game because the ball is commonly hooked through the legs of the loose-head prop (the prop on the left of the scrum nearest to the put-in), which means the opposition scrum half is in a position to apply immediate pressure. One way to alleviate this problem is to position a backline player directly behind the hooker to pick up the ball from the scrum. However, although this may be an effective way of securing possession, it badly affects the width of the attack. Another option is to control the delivery of the ball and ensure it emerges through the *hooker's* legs, which means the attacking scrum half will be slightly further from his opposite number when clearing the ball. To achieve this, the front row should aim to step over the ball in unison, instead of the hooker's conventional strike at the ball. This allows all players to commit to a drive and assume a wide base of support from the beginning of the scrum, better preparing them to withstand the opposition's attempts to disrupt them.

5 BUILDING DEFENCE
A GAME OF STRUCTURE

Defence is all about discipline, not in terms of avoiding giving away penalties, but in terms of players showing the self-restraint and collective control necessary to play to a strict pattern. One defensive error can often result in a try to the opposition, so developing a secure and organised defence is essential.

Defence can be split into two broad areas: pre-tackle and post-tackle. Pre-tackle defence is all about keeping the defensive wall intact and exerting pressure to force the opposition into contact; post-tackle defence is first about contesting possession in contact and then about reconstructing the defensive wall with speed and efficiency. Note that the term defensive *wall* is appropriate because it unmistakably implies something solid and impenetrable.

Pre-tackle defence

Tracking

Tracking is the term used to describe a defender's line of approach to make a tackle, and can determine whether or not the tackle is successful. On a basic level, all defenders should move forwards to take up the attacking team's time and space (see also pages 52–53), but more specifically they should advance on the *inside* of their opponents. If a defender positions directly in front of the ball carrier, his approach has to be cautious to prepare for a break to either side. However, if the defender advances from the inside, the ball carrier will only be able to attack on the outside. This means that the defender can move up more assertively, which should result in a stronger tackle. It is important to note that an inside approach does not mean that the defender should allow the ball carrier to get a long way outside him, just that he should advance in line with the attacker's inside shoulder. There is only a subtle difference in the angle of approach, but it is very effective in narrowing the attacker's running options.

One-on-one defence should be staple practice in a sevens coaching programme. It not only prepares players for a one-on-one situation in a game, but also (and more importantly) enhances a player's competence and contribution when defending within the defensive wall.

The defensive wall

The defensive wall is the basis of a sevens defensive pattern. The main object is not just keeping a level line with the players on the inside and outside, but positioning close enough to one another so that there are no obvious gaps in between. The defensive wall should not try to cover the full width of the pitch all of the time, which is where many teams get it wrong in defence. There is a style of defence called 'zone defence' where each defender covers a channel on the field, but it is a risky pattern because the gaps between players make it easier for the attack to isolate defenders. This style of defence therefore invites attack and can easily be exploited by angled support runners.

In contrast, the defensive wall unites the defenders and significantly narrows the attackers' options. It also deters

COVER INSIDES IN DEFENCE
This is the essence of 7s defence. The defence should move and function as one wall of players. As one player drifts to stay on his man, the player inside him has to move to close any gap that may open up between them. This must happen all the way across the field – the defence must keep moving.

attack by showing the attacking team no immediate chance of making a break (see figure 5.1). The only apparent way to beat the defensive wall is to go around it; this requires a series of quick, long and accurate passes to get the ball out wide before the defenders can cover the space, which is not easy. Defending players should be confident in the knowledge that it is easier to cover a line-break out wide than a break through the centre of the field, because the touchline can be used to narrow the ball carrier's space; however, once a break has been made through the middle, the full width of the field will be available to the attackers, which is a difficult situation for the defence to control.

Another advantage of a tight defensive alignment is that it prevents defenders from becoming isolated. It is not immediately obvious to the attackers which defender is marking whom, making it more difficult for the attack to create and exploit space: after all, an attacker must know who to beat before he can beat him! The defenders, on the other hand, should be absolutely clear who they are marking at all times and communicate this to their team-mates. Most importantly, there should always be a defender nominating the ball carrier.

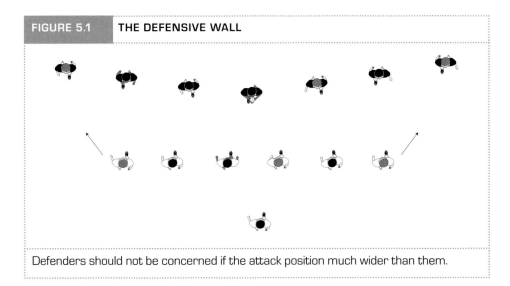

| FIGURE 5.1 | THE DEFENSIVE WALL |

Defenders should not be concerned if the attack position much wider than them.

Sweeper

There is no way around the idea that you have to play with a designated sweeper in defence. The old-fashioned pattern of using wingers to drop back as the ball moves away from them cannot be sustained for very long. There is also no way a player in the middle of the field can drop back during play, as this would leave a hole in the defensive wall. Finally, without any sweeper at all there would be no-one to cover kicks and no last line of defence to slow down breaks. Teams therefore have to play with a sweeper.

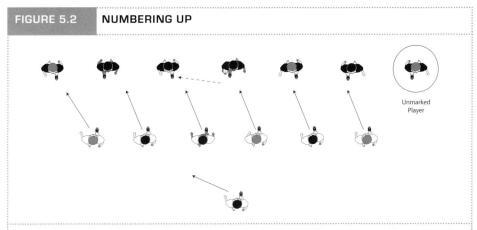

| FIGURE 5.2 | NUMBERING UP |

Unmarked Player

Defenders move across the field as a line, numbering up from the outside and leaving the furthest attacker unmarked.

With a sweeper behind, the defensive wall is made up of six players defending seven attackers, so it must constantly shift and slide to cover the extra attacker. In order to cover the overlap, defenders must count from the outside inwards to identify and nominate the attacker they should be marking. Basically, the last defender covers the last attacker, the second last defender covers the second last attacker and so on. This is called 'numbering up' from the outside (see also pages 18–19). Defenders should identify who they are marking as early as possible and be careful not to over-track, which occurs when a defender runs beyond the inside shoulder of his opponent. There will always be one player left unmarked on the attacking team, and the defence need to ensure that it is the widest player on the opposite side of the field to which the ball is travelling (see figure 5.2). This is a pretty simple concept, but demands a fair bit of practice.

Applying pressure

Since defenders have to constantly slide to cover the attack, they often fall into the habit of moving only laterally and not forwards, which puts inadequate pressure on the attacking team. Players should always aim to act positively in defence, which means *applying* pressure rather than just absorbing it. The idea of defenders moving up in to the passing lanes of the attacking team has been around for a while and is designed to isolate the ball carrier and force him into contact (see figure 5.3). This is advantageous for the defence because every tackle situation should be seen as a chance to contest and regain possession.

FIGURE 5.3	APPLYING PRESSURE IN DEFENCE

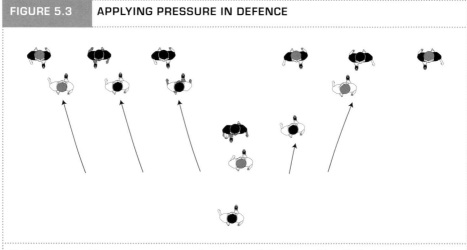

Defenders pushing up into the passing lanes of the opposition limit their options, but this is a risky pattern to employ.

However, this style of defence lacks structure and cohesion and the broken formation presents clear opportunities for the attack to get in behind the defence with angled support runners. Also, when contact is made, offside lines are created and the defenders have to retreat to get back on-side, presenting an opportunity for the attack to run against a disorganised defence. Therefore, the conclusion is that a flat defensive wall is undoubtedly the most effective and efficient system, although the principle of exerting pressure to inhibit attackers should be retained and encouraged. The defending players must take advantage of every opportunity to push forwards.

If the defenders get stretched as the result of a sustained attack and a defending player is unable to reach his opponent, he can be 'saved' by the player outside him. This means that the outside defender leaves the player he is marking and comes in to make the tackle on the ball carrier. The decision to make the save should be made by the outside defenders; inside defenders should always communicate to outside defenders, so if an outside defender does not hear his inside team-mate nominating the ball carrier, he should be immediately aware that there is a problem. The defender who makes the save must change his angle very quickly to kill the attack and allow the ball carrier no time to react. He must also aim to make as aggressive a tackle as possible – and certainly one that prevents any offload – to give the defence a chance to reset their pattern. The practice of outside defenders coming in to make the tackle should generally be avoided at all costs as it breaks the pattern of an inside approach and isolates the defender making the save, but players may need to use it as a last-ditch attempt to prevent a try.

Inside cover

As the defenders track across field to cover a wide attack, it is essential that they keep their inside approach and their tight alignment. As one player moves up and across, the player on his inside must slide simultaneously to close any gap that could open up between them. This is called *inside cover* and should occur seamlessly across the defensive wall. Defenders must work together and aim to move smoothly as one unit rather than as six individuals, almost as if they were connected by equal lengths of cord.

Every defender must understand that he plays a role in keeping the

INSIDE COVER MUST BE SYNCHRONISED

One of the most common errors in defence is when the inside cover gets beaten. Defenders therefore need to be synchronised as they move in to position and cover each inside. If a player forgets to move up and across to cover the inside of the defender outside him, he will have to rush to inside cover if a break is made and will therefore be vulnerable to being sidestepped himself.

defensive wall intact, even if the ball is on the other side of the pitch. Inside cover must extend throughout the team in order to give the defensive wall its solidity. Players must use their own judgement in deciding how close they should be to the defender outside them: they must be close enough to safeguard against a sidestep or a pass to an inside runner, but not so close that the defensive wall is overly compressed. When called upon to make a tackle, the inside cover must treat the situation like a save (see page 53) and be quick to kill the attack to allow the defence time to reorganise.

Inside cover is also essential in covering attacks out wide. If the opposition move the ball wide, the last defender should have total confidence to cover across at speed and trust his inside player to be there to cover him if he is sidestepped. Although he must do his best to maintain a controlled inside approach, it is more important that he ensures the attacker does not beat him on the outside. It is therefore essential that the last defender has the support of a full and tight defensive wall to prevent his man from getting around him (see figure 5.4). It should be considered the responsibility of the whole defensive team to prevent a break out wide, not just the job of one defender.

| FIGURE 5.4 | INSIDE COVER |

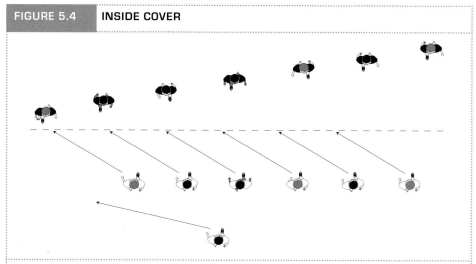

The last defender must be confident to move across at speed and trust his inside cover. All players must stay connected in this situation and force the attackers into contact so the defence can reorganise.

It is not uncommon in sevens to see the defending wing move up very cautiously on his opposite man, clearly wary of being beaten on the outside. However, with committed inside cover the defending wing should be able to advance far more assertively. In fact, the defence should aim to be particularly aggressive when the attack have moved the ball out wide as their attacking options will be far more limited than they are in the middle of the field.

The sweeper has an equally important role in ensuring the defensive wall remains intact and all players apply inside cover. He must be vocal and direct the defenders in front of him to prevent gaps opening up in the defensive wall. He should generally maintain a position in front of the ball and about twenty metres behind his team mates. When a break is made through the line, he should keep the ball carrier on his outside and use the touchline to narrow the attacker's space. He should also move forwards to give the ball carrier less time to weigh up his options, and can try to upset the ball carrier's timing by suddenly changing the pace of his approach.

DON'T GET BEATEN ON THE OUTSIDE

By approaching on the inside shoulder the defender is essentially giving the attacker only one running option, which is to make an outside break. While it is important to protect your inside in defence, it is also important to prevent an outside break. Defenders therefore need to be confident to push out at speed and depend on the player inside to cover a sidestep.

Post-tackle defence

The tackle

A tackler should never have to reach out to tackle the ball carrier. Instead, defenders should use short, quick steps to get their feet close enough to the ball carrier to make sure that initial contact is made with the shoulder rather than with the arms or hands. The idea of an imaginary hula hoop around the feet of the ball carrier is an excellent way of teaching players about effective foot positioning and range. This simple but effective concept works by encouraging the tackler to plant his front foot inside the imaginary hoop just before contact is made. This enables him to stay balanced in the tackle and ensures he is close enough to make firm shoulder contact. Safety must be emphasised in all contact situations and players should be instructed to keep their head slightly to the side and their spine in the correct alignment.

The contact point on the ball carrier must also be considered. Tackles around the thighs are less effective in sevens than in the 15-a-side game as they allow the ball carrier to keep his arms free and offload the ball to a support runner. In sevens, the need to stop the ball moving must always be factored in to the execution of the tackle; players should understand that it is more advantageous to drive the shoulder in *above* the level of the ball to prevent an immediate offload and then work on putting the ball carrier to ground. Defenders should wrap and squeeze their arms around the ball carrier to keep their shoulder pinned to the player and avoid falling off the tackle. Another option is for the defender to hook the front leg of the ball carrier and lift it off the ground, which will eliminate his power. The defender should also maintain his leg drive throughout contact to try to drive the ball carrier backwards, which will further disrupt the presentation and transfer of the ball. This kind of tackle may not always be possible, especially if the ball carrier has a strong fend, but players must retain the idea of stopping both the man and the ball in every tackle.

The goal in defence is not just to stop the attack, but always to win back the ball. Within the defensive wall, defenders should communicate and cooperate in pairs (chiefly with the player on their inside) to apply pressure and contest possession. For example, when a player nominates the ball carrier there should be immediate dialogue between him and his inside cover. Similarly, when contact is made the inside cover should get involved, either to assist in the tackle if the ball carrier is still moving forwards or to try to steal the ball if the tackle is complete. If he chooses to assist in the tackle, it is vital that he kills the attack and prevents the ball carrier from passing out of the tackle. To steal the ball he should simply step over the tackled player, grab the ball, then look to clear the ball from pressure.

However, the opposition will often be quick to support the tackled player and their primary support player will usually hold over the ball to provide a shield for the scrum half to pass the ball away (see page 31). A neat tactic in this situation is to break off from contesting for the ball for a moment, then drive the bridging player just as the scrum half picks up the ball. This can either disrupt his handling or force a knock-on. Another option is to pull the bridging player through to release the ball from the ruck. The defender must always weigh up his chances of success before committing to the tackle contest because, at times, it may be a better option to let the opposition have the ball and the defence to focus on re-establishing the defensive wall.

DEFENCE PATTERNS START AGAIN AFTER EVERY TACKLE

Encourage players to work from one tackle situation to the next. Every tackle is a contest for possession, and the aim is to force the opposition into contact for a chance to challenge for the ball. The players must communicate and be active to re-establish defensive patterns following a tackle.

England's Henry Paul and Dave Strettle deny USA's Mike Palefau a chance to offload the ball in the tackle.

Reorganising the defensive wall

Every time there is a tackle, the defenders have to reposition as they reorganise the defensive wall. They have to consider offside lines, assess where the attack are likely to strike next and nominate who they are marking. However, the most important aim following a tackle is for the defence to match the number of attackers on either side of the ruck (see figure 5.5). This is possible even when the defence employ a sweeper and are effectively playing six-up against seven. It is essential that the defenders are aggressive and disruptive in contact to force the attack to commit three players to the tackle situation, which then gives the defence the chance to equate numbers exactly.

FIGURE 5.5   REPOSITIONING FOLLOWING A TACKLE

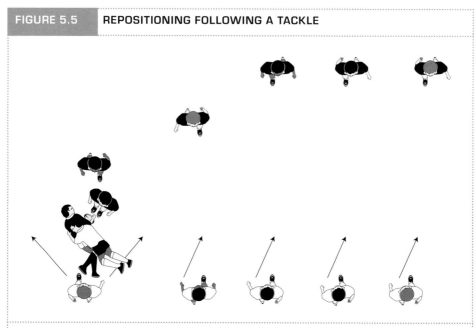

Defenders must communicate and show urgency to match the number of attackers on either side of the ruck.

It is also critical that there is never more than one defender on the floor – the tackler – and this player should try to get back to his feet as quickly as possible, certainly before his opponent. The tackler's inside cover *must* stay on his feet, whether he assists in the tackle or contests possession. His determined contest for possession must slow down the delivery of the ball from the ruck; this will give the defenders more time to reorganise and restart the defensive pattern. If he has been unable to win the ball in the tackle contest, he should take up a position very close behind the ruck, on guard for a run from the attacking scrum half. Once the scrum half passes, he should move up into the defensive wall.

All defending players must be quick to react to a tackle; if not, they will present clear opportunities to the attack. The most effective way to organise any defensive pattern with speed and efficiency is for players to communicate, and this must be emphasised in tackle situations. A tackle should always trigger urgent

POST-TACKLE WORK RATE

Players have to consciously increase their effort following a tackle in terms of their concentration, communication and organisation. Defending players need to count and identify who they should be marking as quickly as possible, and re-activate their defensive line.

communication, and all players should be vocal and enthusiastic in organising a new defensive wall. In particular, it is important that those defenders *not* involved in the tackle communicate and direct those who are and those who are closest to the ruck.

The defence should actively compress following a tackle to facilitate communication and to stop an immediate break around the edge of the ruck. The defenders have to resist the temptation to stand opposite the more widely positioned attackers; as long as each defender identifies and nominates who they are marking, there is no need for them to be concerned about their apparent lack of width. The rules of the defensive wall should be reapplied, such that the last defender covers the last attacker and so on (see pages 50–52). Players should be encouraged to consciously reset and restart the defensive pattern at every tackle situation. This gives the defenders clear goals and a framework within which to work.

When a turnover is won, the defenders need to work quickly to take advantage of the situation. The sweeper should immediately move up and aim to enter the attacking line as a first receiver. The depth of his position will have allowed him to assess the opposition's alignment and make a good decision about how and where to attack. If the ball comes out before the sweeper has had time to move up, he should move to support the inside of the first receiver to give him the option of running an attacking movement pattern with an inside runner. There is often little point in spinning the ball out wide after a turnover because the opposition will be positioned considerably wider, as they will have been expecting to maintain possession. The ball carrier and support players must move quickly to take advantage of the space between their opponents and look to penetrate the line as early as possible, before the opposition have time to organise their defence.

Defending from a scrum

There are numerous considerations when defending from a scrum. The most immediate concern involves the players in the scrum itself. Primarily, the forwards' aim is to drive their opponents off the ball, but it is important that they weigh up their chances of success before taking this option. Players who focus totally on a drive will be slower to break from the scrum, leaving the team defensively exposed if the opposition win the ball and are able to play it quickly. If they are up against a much stronger unit, the defending scrum should instead look to disrupt delivery of the ball by wheeling the scrum or pulling straight back. Both methods aim to force an uncontrolled delivery of the ball, which can be immediately contested by the scrum half.

The scrum half's first job is to hustle his opposite number for the ball. Scrums in sevens are generally messy affairs, so the defending scrum half often has a good chance of getting hold of his man with the ball. After pressuring his opponent, the scrum half's job is then to cover space to defend any immediate break.

Right-field scrum

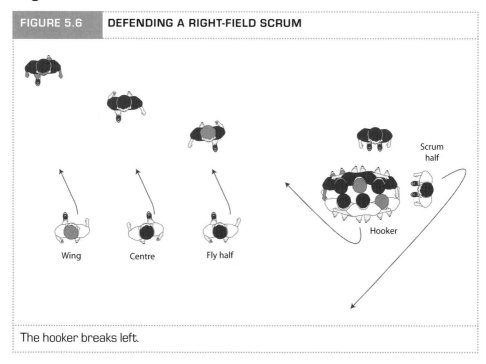

FIGURE 5.6   DEFENDING A RIGHT-FIELD SCRUM

Scrum half

Hooker

Wing   Centre   Fly half

The hooker breaks left.

In a right-field scrum, the scrum half holds his position to cover any attack to his right, then drops back to sweep.

The hooker breaks left from every scrum, so from a right-field scrum he moves quickly to cover the inside of the fly half. In set pieces, the hooker plays a crucial role in establishing the defensive wall with the backline as quickly as possible. The props should therefore always try to bind on each other and not the hooker, if the referee allows it, in order to facilitate a quicker exit for the hooker (see also pages 46–47).

Backline defence from a scrum is all about running the defensive pattern. It is important that the backline move up quickly but not wildly, so that their approach is controlled. In a right-field scrum, the fly half must stay alert for a break from the attacking scrum half before advancing on to his opposite man (see figure 5.6). It is the hooker's responsibility to let the fly half know as soon as he is in position, so that the fly half can move up with confidence to cover his own man.

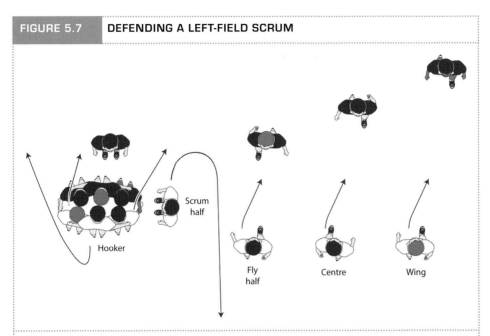

FIGURE 5.7   **DEFENDING A LEFT-FIELD SCRUM**

The scrum half covers the inside of the fly half before dropping back to take up his sweeping position.

Left-field scrum

From a left-field scrum, the scrum half has a busy role to fulfil. After hustling his opposite number for the ball, he must cover the inside of the fly half and take up an immediate but temporary position in the defensive line before dropping back to sweep (see figure 5.7). The obvious danger here is that he will leave a gap when he drops out of the line, so it is essential that he does not drop back until his position in the defensive line has been taken over by the prop. The prop must communicate this to the scrum half.

Another concern with this pattern is that if the scrum half is caught up in a tackle while in the defensive line, the defending team will have no sweeper. The hooker again breaks left from the scrum to cover the attacking scrum half running to that side. It is unrealistic to expect the loose head prop to cover this space as quickly as the hooker because he is bound to an opponent who may deliberately hold him in the scrum. Despite modified laws that forbid the hooker binding underneath the props shoulders (see pages 46–47), the hooker is still the quickest player to cover the blindside of a left-field scrum.

An alternative option is for the scrum half to swap positions with the hooker for a left-field scrum; after the scrum is over, the scrum half quickly breaks left to cover an attack down the blindside. This is arguably a safer position from which to drop back and sweep. The hooker will fill the role of applying pressure on the opposition scrum half, before maintaining his familiar position in the defensive wall inside the fly half. The scrum half may not be as strong in the scrum as the hooker, but this could be factored in to the selection criteria for his position.

Defending a lineout

There are very few lineouts in sevens, but defending players must still be given clear and defined roles for this area of the game. The scrum half has the simplest job: he stands in the 5 m channel so that he can move into his sweeping position quickly. The backline also have relatively straightforward orders to run the usual defensive pattern, but the fly half plays a major role in communicating to the forwards in order to establish the defensive wall as quickly as possible.

The forwards should position in a way to first contest possession and then move into the defensive pattern. The two props stand in the lineout and team up

FIGURE 5.8	DEFENDING A LINEOUT

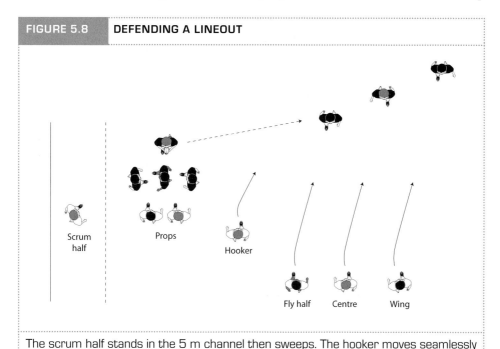

The scrum half stands in the 5 m channel then sweeps. The hooker moves seamlessly in to the defensive line.

to challenge for the ball. Their main option is a one-man lift, which is an effective and efficient way of putting pressure on the opposition throw. The technique is simple but requires practice. The jumper should move forwards towards the throw, with the lifter in front of him. The lifter should have a wide base for balance and stability and bend at the knees to maximise the leg strength, and should also get in as tight as possible to the jumper and reach full extension. The defenders should *not* copy the attack and use two players to support a jumper to contest for the ball in the air; this would commit all defending forwards to the jump and delay their movement into the defensive pattern, presenting clear opportunities for the attacking scrum half to run into the space created around the lineout.

The hooker stands at the back and slightly out of the lineout in the scrum half position. He covers the possibility of an overthrow and deters the opposition scrum half from running around the back of the lineout. By being at the back of the lineout he will also be in his familiar position and be able to quickly link up with the fly half to establish the defensive wall (see figure 5.8).

All players should be encouraged to move forwards in defence. The defending forwards in a lineout often have a tendency to cover across to the open side of the field too early, which leaves the defence vulnerable to a playback (see pages 40–42). Players in the lineout should move forwards first and then across as they form the defensive wall. They should also regularly observe the alignment and body language of the opponents in front of them and be prepared for a sudden attack back towards their side of the field.

6 RESTARTS

A GAME OF STRUCTURE

Kick-offs

Kicking team

There are two main options for the kicking team at kick-off – a high, short kick on the 10 m line or high, long kick down the 15 m channel. The consistent factor is the height of the kick: it must be as high as possible to give the chasers a chance to contest for the ball in the air. The option of a little grubber kick just over the 10 m line can be taken if the opposition are way out of position, but this is usually a spontaneous decision made by the kicker rather than a planned tactic.

It is imperative that the kicker is able to kick the ball where desired, either short or long. This takes extensive practice, but the main piece of advice to give the kicker is to 'watch your foot strike the ball'. This is a remarkably simple concept, but most poor kicks are a result of the kicker failing to keep his eye on the ball at the crucial moment when boot strikes ball. The kicker should also drop the ball from a height no higher than his knee to be sure of a controlled drop. It is then down to practice and developing a personal system that can be repeated with consistent success. However, a kick is only as good as the chase, and team roles at the kick-off need to be developed in training.

Short kick-off

Option 1 (see figure 6.1(a)) is an offensive chasing pattern that applies maximum pressure on the opposition, yet also serves to position the players in a tight defensive alignment in case the ball is lost. All of the players have specific roles in the pattern.

Players 1 and 3 are the designated jumpers whose aim is to contest the ball in the air. During their approach it is essential that they communicate to agree on a course of action, which will be determined by the state of the kick. If it is a good kick, one of them should jump for it while the other slows his approach and falls in directly behind the jump to field a tap-back. If it is a poor kick, neither may jump, with the players instead choosing to initially target the opposition catcher rather than the ball: one makes a smother-tackle and the other works for the turnover.

Player 2 advances *beyond* the ball to intercept any tap-back between the opposition catcher and his support.

FIGURE 6.1(A) SHORT KICK-OFF – OPTION 1

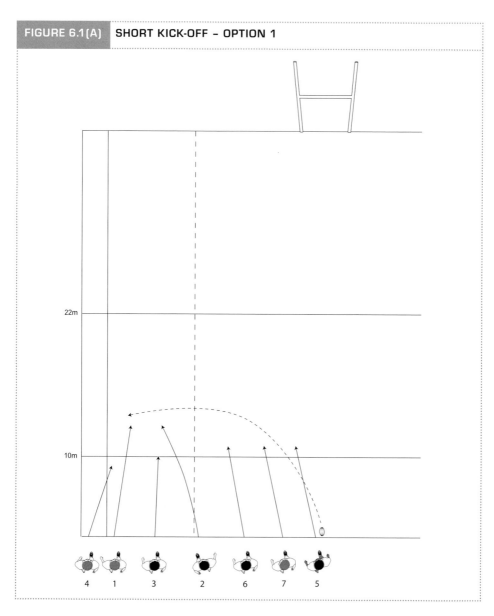

Player 4, the scrum half, initially moves up to cover any immediate attacks to the blindside, and will then be in a safe position to retreat to his sweeping role. He will also be close enough to contribute to the attack if the ball is won in the air.

Players 5, 6 and 7 are integral in establishing the defensive line in midfield and must advance quickly to cut off a long pass infield, which then forces the opposition into contact.

Another option, and a good way to gain an advantage, is to play away from opposition strength. This can be done by swapping the positions of the forwards and backs in the line-up, so the backs are nearest the touchline shaping up to chase the kick and the forwards are positioned nearest to the kicker (see figure 6.1(b)).

| FIGURE 6.1(B) | SHORT KICK-OFF – OPTION 2 |

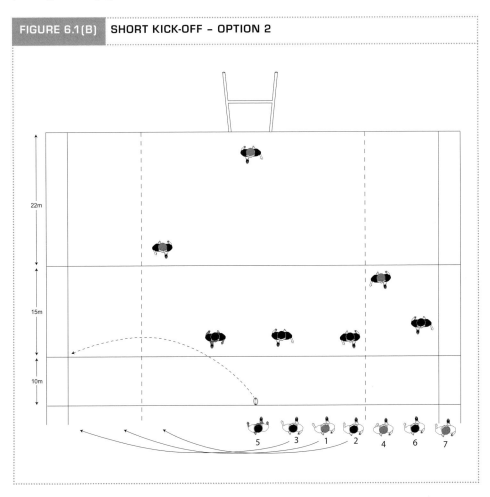

On a signal, the forwards run behind the kicker to the other side of the field and prepare to chase. There will be no time for the opposition forwards to get across and reposition in time, which means that the chasing team will be jumping against fewer players (who will also usually be less practised in fielding kick-offs). The risk is that, if the ball is lost, the kicking team will spread across the field with no defensive wall in place.

Long kick-off

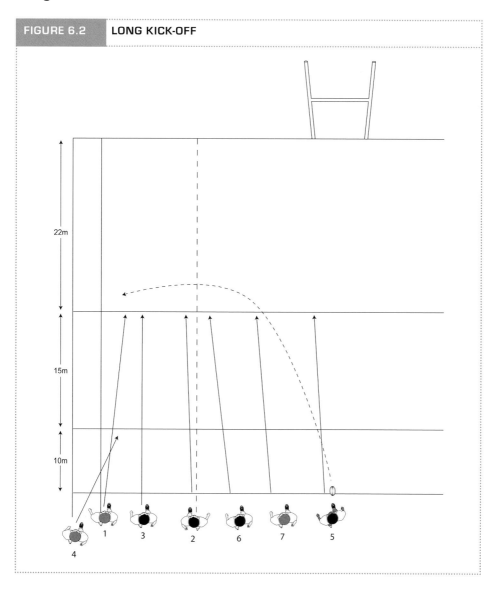

FIGURE 6.2   **LONG KICK-OFF**

Roles at a long kick-off are a little more uniform, since it is expected that the other team will win the ball. All players push up in a defensive wall, except the scrum half who holds a deep position to cover any kicks (see figure 6.2). The kicker should still aim to loft the ball as high as possible at a long kick-off to give his team a chance to exert immediate pressure on the opposition, forcing them to kick or take contact. Often, teams chasing long kick-offs have an incongruous tendency to advance more slowly than at a short kick-off, even though they have more ground to cover. This is the wrong approach and just gives the opposition more time to clear the ball to space and plan their attack. Players have to be encouraged to move up as quickly as is possible and maintain the defensive wall.

Receiving team

FIGURE 6.3	POSITIONS OF THE RECEIVING TEAM AT A KICK-OFF

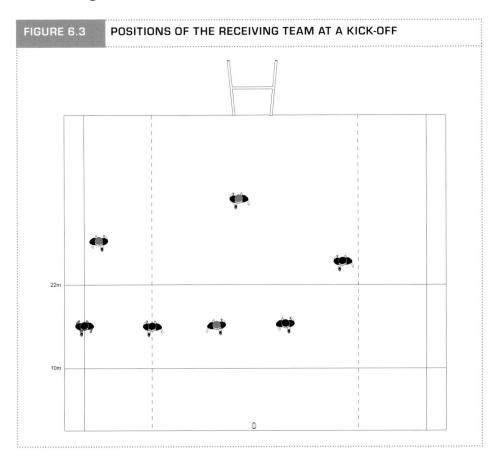

The receiving team must be positioned to ensure adequate coverage of the field. The most efficient formation is 4-up, 3-back, as shown in figure 6.3. Players should stand a couple of metres back from where they expect the ball to descend, so that they can run on to the ball keeping it and the opposition in view at all times.

As soon as the kick has been taken, players must communicate and organise a support unit to ensure possession is secured and maintained when the ball is caught. From short kick-offs, players should aim to make a clean catch and then clear the ball from pressure as quickly as possible. As he lands, the catcher must dynamically turn towards his team-mates, sink at the knees and establish a wide base of support to withstand impact, then use shoulder rolls and elbows to prevent the opposition from slowing down the ball. If the defence rush up and block the passing lanes, the ball carrier should target the space behind the defenders and look to offload to angled support runners. He may also need to take contact to establish offside lines and force the opposition to retreat, and then try to recycle the ball quickly.

Long kick-offs present more of an opportunity for a counterattack as the catcher will not be under such immediate pressure. The ball should be moved quickly to the fly half in the middle of the field, who can then link up with his centre and wing to execute the attacking movement patterns (see pages 13–24). Moving the ball wide from a long kick-off serves to stretch the defence to facilitate line breaks, but it also flattens the attacking line; therefore, players have to work extra hard to get back behind the ball and attain good depth and alignment in order to attack.

22 m drop-outs

Kicking team

22 m drop-outs happen far less frequently in sevens than in the 15-a-side game, but a system still needs to be developed to ensure the kicking team retain the ball. As soon as the ball is touched down behind the try line, players should move quickly to the 22 m line to be in position to take a quick drop-out. The ball should be given to a player with no defender in front of him, and this player should aim to take the kick before the defence have time to organise. The kicker's first priority is always to take a little drop kick to himself, staying low over the ball to maximise control; it is important that all players in the team are able to execute this type of kick. Support players must then react quickly to give the ball carrier an immediate option to pass.

The kicker can still take a short kick to himself even if the defence are well organised and have covered an attempt to take the kick quickly. The execution is simple: the kicker stays very low over his drop kick, then immediately throws the ball back through his legs to the scrum half to avoid a tackle contest and retain possession. The scrum half stands in a deeper position for this purpose, as shown in figure 6.4, then looks to strike at the defence with the attacking movement patterns (see pages 13–24).

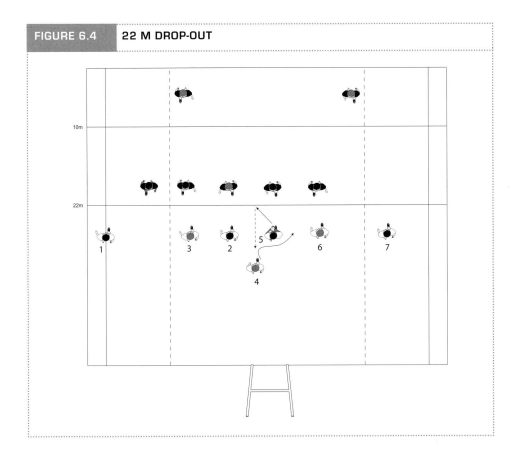

FIGURE 6.4 22 M DROP-OUT

Another option is to kick long down the 15 m channels with an organised defensive wall in pursuit. This may surrender possession, but a good chase can exert considerable pressure on the opposition. It is imperative that the chasing team maintain a tight defensive wall and aim to advance more quickly than their opponents, who will be working to get back behind the ball to join the attack.

Receiving team

The priority when receiving a 22 m drop-out is to stop the opposition from taking the drop kick quickly, thus giving the defence more time to organise. Five players spread across the 22 m line to cover the short kick, with two players deep in sweeping roles to cover the long kick (see figure 6.4). When the ball has been caught, the other players should quickly form into a support unit to ensure successful continuity.

Options at a penalty or free kick

Making the right choice at a penalty can mean the difference between winning and losing and a split-second decision is often needed to seize the initiative. Various factors influence this decision, such as field position, the score line, the amount of time left in the game and the state of the defence. Whatever decision is taken, players need to show both urgency and composure to make sure an opportunity to score is not squandered.

The most common options at a penalty are a quick tap, a kick at goal, a kick for touch or running a set move. From free kicks, the options are limited to a quick tap or the set moves on pages 74–7.

KICK BACK KICKS

The easiest and simplest way to field a kick in 7s, although possibly the least adventurous, is to kick it back. Some may argue that possession is everything, but it is far better to defend with all of your players in the right place to defend than with all of your players in front of the ball in attack.

A quick tap is often the preferred choice from penalties and free kicks as it gives the attack an opportunity to run against a disorganised and retreating defence, although a common problem with this is that the ball carrier can dart off and isolate himself from his support, nullifying the advantage of the penalty. However, the expectation should be for support players to keep up with the ball carrier, not for the ball carrier to slow down for support. Support players must therefore aim to react simultaneously when a penalty is awarded and start communicating to the ball carrier and directing play immediately. The attacking movement patterns on pages 13–24 are particularly effective from a quick tap.

Alternatively, the team can run the following set moves. They can be used anywhere on the field, but are most deadly close to the opposition try line. Their design is based on manipulating the movement of the defence. A good defence should close the attack down very quickly to disrupt their timing, yet teams defending set penalty moves often adopt a much more cautious approach and their first movement is usually sideways. The defensive line may be well organised, but it often advances with little conviction, which just gives the attack more time and space to run their move.

It is important that players are able to adjust during set penalty moves to accommodate an unexpected defensive pattern. Players should be constantly assessing the defence and making decisions, not just robotically running pre-determined lines. The movements of players off the ball in these set penalty moves give the ball carrier a variety of options, so he must keep an open mind and, with one eye on the defence, pick his runner.

Set move 1

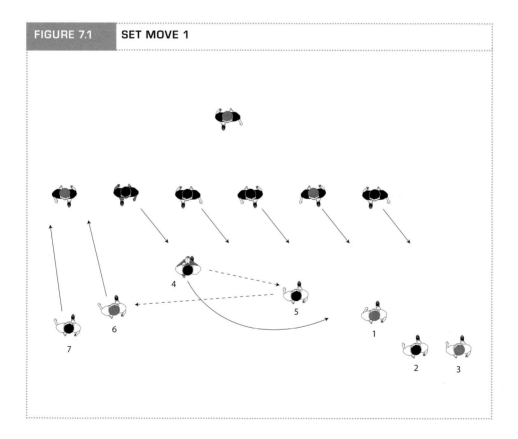

FIGURE 7.1	SET MOVE 1

Set move 1 aims to create a clear two-on-one situation as quickly as possible. The move specifically exploits the six-man defensive line, where the last attacker is left unmarked. The scrum half (player 4) makes a long pass to the fly half (5) and then loops around him, forcing the defence to slide across to cover. If the defence number up exactly, the fly half should make a long flat pass back to the two players on the other side of the pitch (6 and 7), who can execute a two-on-one on the last defender (see figure 7.1). If the defence do not slide, the fly half will also have the option to use the overlap outside him.

Set move 2

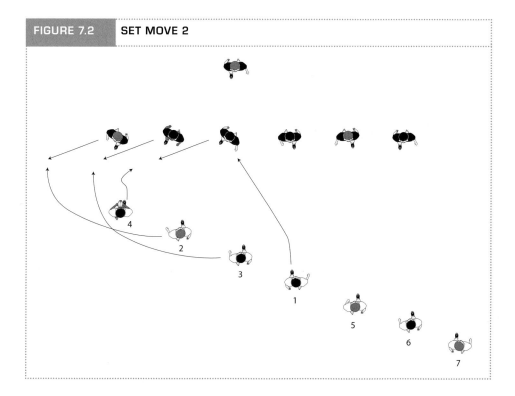

FIGURE 7.2 | SET MOVE 2

Set move 2 is designed for a penalty or free kick on the left- or right-hand side of the pitch. The attacking movement, which can be played as either a strike or a playback (see pages 33–42), again exploits the idea that the defenders have to number up from the outside, and tests their inside cover. The alignment is shown in figure 7.2: the scrum half (player 4) is on the ball with the three forwards outside him, then the backline unit. The movement begins when the scrum half places the ball on the floor, which is the signal for the two forwards outside him

(1 and 2) to run around him as fast as possible. It will not be difficult for the defenders to cover these two players, but their movement will stretch the defence and open up gaps. The scrum half should look and run towards the looping players, then step in suddenly to fix his marker. He then plays an inside ball to the third forward in line (3), who has timed an angled run. As a strike, this player should hit the ball at full pace and slice through the defensive line; as a playback, he should run with control and pace to immediately pop the ball straight back to the scrum half, who loops around him like in a 'You-and-me' (see pages 18–20).

Set move 3

FIGURE 7.3	SET MOVE 3

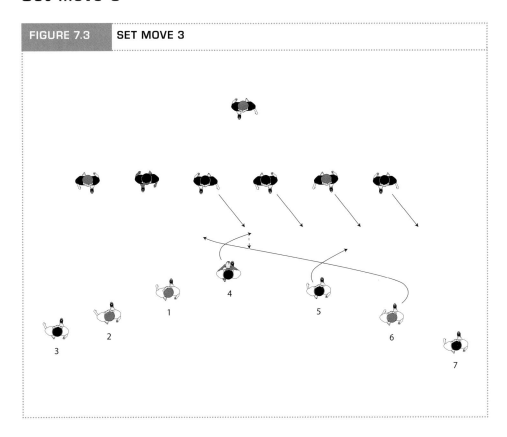

Set move 3 is specifically for penalties or free kicks around the middle of the field, and also works on the principle of moving defenders to create space to attack.

The scrum half (player 4) starts with the ball between two units of three players. He assesses the defence and targets the side with more space and fewer defenders. The players outside him initially mirror his angle of run, which will pull the defenders across the pitch. The player in the centre of the attacking backline or forward unit (player 6 or 2) then changes his angle sharply and runs a late switch with the scrum half (see figure 7.3). He should either break the line himself or look to link up with the players in the other attacking unit. The alignment for this set penalty move 2 allows for endless attacking possibilities, including all of the attacking movement patterns used in open play (see pages 13–24).

PART 2
DRILLS

8 ATTACK DRILLS

DRILL Channel passing

SKILL
Handling: The ability to make a long pass is essential.

SETUP
1 ball between 3 players (groups of 4 or 5 are also possible).

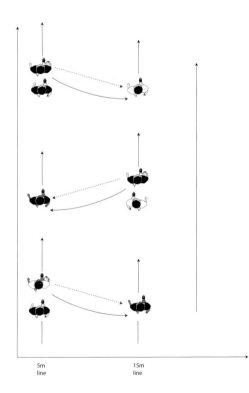

5m
line

15m
line

DESCRIPTION

The drill is performed up the full length of the field on the 5 m and 15 m lines. In groups of three, each player passes, follows his pass and falls in behind the receiver. If players are initially not capable of a 10 m pass, the drill can be performed up the touchline and the 5 m line.

COACHING POINTS

- The spin pass is the fastest kind of pass. Use the top hand to give power and spin and the bottom hand to provide direction.
- Pass in front of the receiver at chest height.
- The receiver should hold up his hands as a target for the pass.
- Aim to run at pace and complete as many passes as possible.

DRILL   Quick hands

SKILL
Handling: Players need to be able to pass accurately under pressure.

SETUP
- 1 ball between 3 players
- 4 cones marking out a 10 m² grid

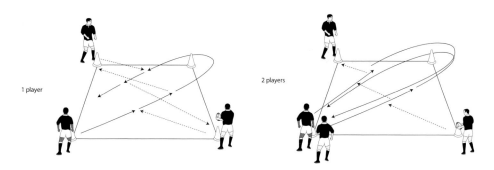

1 player

2 players

DESCRIPTION

Player runs diagonally across the grid and receives the ball from a player positioned on one corner of the grid. He then passes it across the grid to another stationary player. After passing, the player runs around the marker ahead of him and returns to the starting point, performing the skill again on his way back.

COACHING POINTS

- Run in a straight line.
- Extend the hands to catch the ball early and watch the ball into the hands.
- Communicate on every pass.

PROGRESSIONS

- Perform the drill on a 20 m² grid.
- Players could run in pairs across a larger grid, as shown above.

DRILL   Depth

SKILL	SETUP
Realignment: Players must consider their alignment and depth.	• 1 ball between 12 players • 6 cones marking out a 20 m × 15 m grid, with two pass/place markers (as shown)

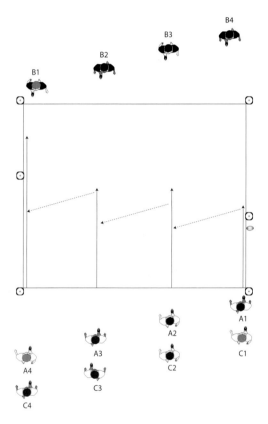

DESCRIPTION

In fours, the players align with sufficient depth to pick up the ball at one marker and place it at the other. The first player (A1) passes the ball from the pass/place marker to start the drill and the other players pass the ball swiftly along the line. The last man must have enough time and space to place the ball on the second pass/place marker on the run, without having to stop or check his run.

As soon as the ball has been placed, the next team of four begin. Players change positions after every repetition.

COACHING POINTS

• Start with the outside foot forwards.

• Accelerate on to the ball and run in a straight line.

• Receivers should have their inside hand out as a target for the passer.

• Passers should turn their head quickly to locate the target. This facilitates a quicker transfer of the ball across the body.

PROGRESSION

The drill can be made more difficult by putting the pass/place markers more in line with each other so the team have less time in which to pass the ball across the grid.

DRILL   Up 'n' backs

SKILL	SETUP
Realignment: Players must be able to realign quickly.	• 2 balls between 10 players • 6 cones marking out a grid 15–20 m wide by 10–12 m long and 2 cones showing the defenders' positions

DESCRIPTION

An 'up 'n' back' is simply the practice of passing a ball along a line of four players through a grid and back again. Players take it in turns to be the working pair (the two middle players in the line of four). Two defenders stand in the centre of the grid and must stay on their markers. Their aim is just to reach out to knock the ball.

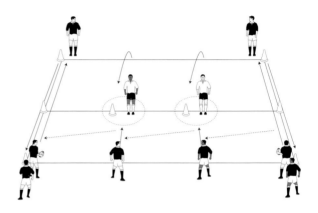

The working pair run continuously for a set number of repetitions. The other players run one length each in relay. The drill requires two balls – one on either side of the grid – as shown above. After every up 'n' back, the ball that is in play is placed by the marker and the ball from the other side of the grid is used. This ensures that the players develop their passing off both hands. The working pair become the defenders once they have completed their set.

COACHING POINTS

• Players should align deep enough to ensure the defenders do not block a pass and to allow acceleration on to the ball.

• Pass at chest height in front of the receiver.

• Extend the hands to receive the ball.

• Run in a straight line.

PROGRESSION

Allow the defenders to move laterally to test the attackers' ability to run straight.

DRILL   Depth square

SKILL
Realignment: The depth must be just right for success.

SETUP
- 2 balls between 8 players
- 4 cones marking out a 20 m² grid

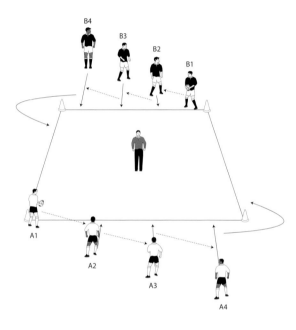

DESCRIPTION

In fours, players work around the outside of the grid as shown in the diagram. The ball is passed along the line of players as they run towards the edge of the grid; the aim is for the last player to receive the ball before crossing the border of the grid and then place the ball on the corner cone. The four players then move around the grid and realign. On the coach's whistle, the teams change direction.

COACHING POINTS

- The 1st receiver (A2/B2) must set the depth for the team – the depth of this player will determine the success of the drill.
- Receivers should show their inside hand as a target for the pass.
- Passes must be accurate and thrown in front of the receiver so he does not have to check his run to catch the ball.
- Accelerate on to the ball and run straight until after the pass has been made, then chase the pass in support.
- Realign quickly to ensure a quick ball can be used.

PROGRESSION

Introduce one or two defenders who can only move laterally on each side of the grid.

DRILL Traffic

SKILL
Communication: Communication makes the game easier.

SETUP
- 4 balls between 8 or more players
- 4 cones marking out a 10 m² grid and 1 cone marking the centre point

DESCRIPTION

Players line up behind each cone with a ball in every corner. Players have to pick up the ball, run out to the centre marker and then run to any other marker to deliver the ball to the next player in line, but are not allowed to return to the marker they first ran from. Two players cannot run to the same maker, so if this happens one will have to turn back and find another marker that is free. Players wait on their markers and do not go out to meet the pass.

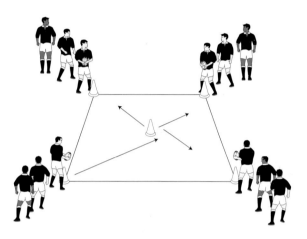

COACHING POINTS

- Players should get rid of the ball as quickly as possible. Communication from all players – both those with the ball and those on the markers – will help to achieve this.
- Players should not stop moving in the grid, so if there is no opportunity to get rid of the ball they should slow down and accelerate when there is an open marker.

PROGRESSIONS

- Introduce various conditions, for example players are not allowed to run to the marker directly ahead of their own.
- Give a ball to one of the players at a corner; this player then enters the grid and the drill continues with five balls.

DRILL   Talk early

SKILL
Communication: Players should direct play through constant and early communication.

SETUP
- 1 ball between 9 or more players
- 4 cones marking out a 15 m² grid

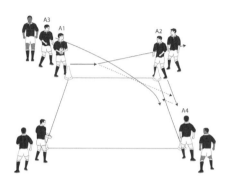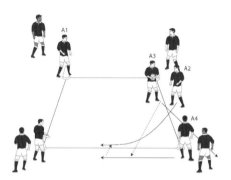

DESCRIPTION

Players position on each corner and perform the drill around the edge of the grid. A1 runs clockwise and makes a long pass diagonally across the grid to A2, who has also run clockwise from his marker. A3 follows the ball and takes a short inside pass from A2. A3 then makes a long diagonal pass across the grid to A4, A2 follows the ball and takes the short inside pass from A4 and so on around the grid. The drill is continuous, so after every long pass, the passer joins the line of players behind the marker he has passed towards.

COACHING POINTS

- Run with the ball in two hands and pass with the outside hand.
- Catch the ball with the hands out and fingers spread.
- Get rid of the ball as quickly as possible; this demands early communication and concentration from all players.
- Run on to the inside passes at full pace.

PROGRESSION

Introduce a second ball; the balls start at diagonally opposite corners.

DRILL   Timing the step

SKILL	SETUP
Evasion: Defenders running across field at pace are vulnerable to a sidestep.	• 1 ball between 2 or more players • 4 cones marking out a 10 m² grid and 2 cones marking out the starting positions

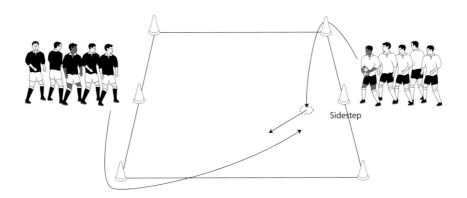

Sidestep

DESCRIPTION

Players line up on either side of the grid. One side are attackers, the other side are defenders. The ball carrier chooses which marker to run around, left or right, and the defender runs around the marker at the opposite end of the grid. The ball carrier should then run straight down the line to force the defender across to cover, and then try to sidestep the defender and score a try at the end of the grid. The defender aims to tackle the ball carrier and prevent a score. Whether or not a try is scored, the defender joins the attackers' line and vice versa and the drill continues with the next two players.

COACHING POINTS

- Ball carrier should run at pace to stretch the defender.
- Execute the sidestep just out of arm's reach from the defender.
- Use a two-step sidestep to fake the direction of attack and shift the defender's balance to one side (see pages 5–6).
- Maintain speed and accelerate with the angle change.
- Run straight lines and sharp angles rather than arcing runs, which give the defender a better chance to adjust.

DRILL   3-man snake

SKILL	**SETUP**
Support: Players should coordinate in threes.	• 1 ball between 3 players • 10 cones marking out a 10 m wide channel, as shown in the diagram

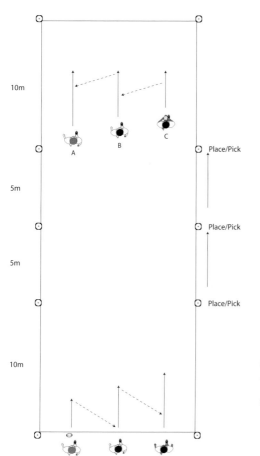

DESCRIPTION

Three players start running through the channel, passing the ball. C places the ball on the first marker; B picks it up and places it on the second marker; A picks it up and places it on the third marker. C then picks up the ball and passes it back to B, who then passes back to A. The three players should realign quickly and move the ball back through the hands to finish.

COACHING POINTS

• Perform the drill at full pace.

• Call instructions to teammates.

• Maintain speed when placing and picking up the ball with two hands.

PROGRESSION

Two teams can race each other down either side of the channel.

DRILL   2v1 continuous

SKILL
Support: All players must be able to identify and execute a two-on-one situation consistently and successfully.

SETUP
- 1 ball between 3 players
- 6 cones per 3 players, marking out grids over a line with all cones around 6 m apart

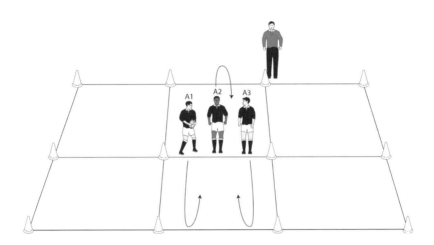

DESCRIPTION

Three players numbered 1, 2 and 3 stand on the centre line of each grid, passing a ball between them. Whichever number the coach calls becomes the defender (if this player is holding the ball when his number is called, he passes it to another player). The defender runs to one end of the grid and returns to defend. The attackers run to the opposite end and then attack, aiming to score a try at the end of the grid. The defender aims to effect a tackle with a two-handed tag on the ball carrier, or to knock down the pass.

COACHING POINTS

- The ball carrier should fix the defender by running at pace and thus create space for the support player.
- Throw a flat well-timed pass so the defender is unable to cover the receiver or knock down the pass.
- Accelerate in to the space.

DRILL   2v1 outside-inside

SKILL
Support: The final pass to put a player through the defence is essential and must be developed.

SETUP
• 1 ball between 4 players
• 7 cones marking out a grid, as shown in the diagram

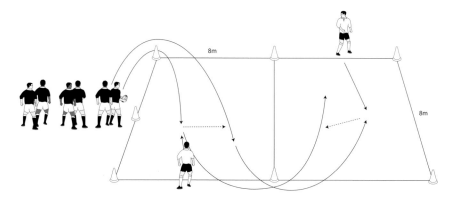

DESCRIPTION

The grid is split into two channels, with a defender at the end of each one. Two attackers enter the grid around a marker and aim to beat the defender in each channel. The first pass should be an outside pass, the second an inside pass. As soon as the support player receives the first pass, he should run to the end of the first channel, turn around the marker and immediately run to attack the other defender with the second attacker in support. The defenders aim to effect a tackle with a two-handed tag on the ball carrier, or to knock down the pass.

COACHING POINTS

• Speed is essential in this drill. Run with pace and purpose to draw and fix defenders.
• Outside passes must be flat to get behind the defender; inside passes must be deeper to avoid interception.
• It is the support player's responsibility to be in position to receive the pass, not the ball carrier's job to slow down for support.
• Run an angle towards the ball on the inside pass to get behind the isolated defender.

DRILL   3v1v1v1 fast-break

SKILL

Support: Support players must be quick to support a player who makes a break.

SETUP

• 1 ball between 6 players
• 8 cones marking out a 5 m wide channel; the cones should be 5 m apart but can be further apart for junior or novice players

DESCRIPTION

Three attackers run around a corner marker and support each other through the channel; three defenders run around markers at different distances to stagger the pressure on the attack, as shown in the diagram. The defenders aim to effect a tackle with a two-handed tag on the ball carrier, or to knock down the pass. The attackers should aim to fix and draw the defenders and use outside and inside passes to beat them. After each drill, the attackers become defenders and vice versa.

COACHING POINTS

• This drill demands quick support play and simulates fast-breaking support after a line-break.

• The ball carrier should create space for support players by running at a defender to fix him or running into space to draw him away.

• Support players should communicate their position to the ball carrier.

• All players should anticipate the play, see the space and accelerate into it.

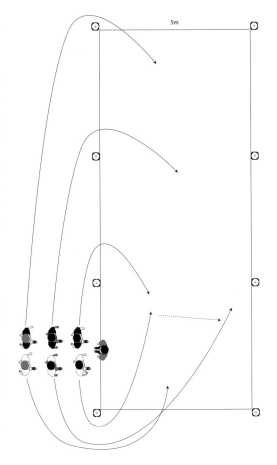

DRILL 4v2 keep-ball

SKILL	SETUP
Support: Players must be comfortable with the ball under pressure.	• 1 ball between 6 players • 4 cones marking out a 15 m² grid (the grid can be smaller for novice players to play 3v1 keep-ball).

DESCRIPTION

The four attackers can run and pass in any direction. If the two defenders tag the ball carrier or recover a dropped ball, or if the attacking team run out of the grid, the defenders swap roles with two of the attackers.

COACHING POINTS

- Move the ball to players in space and away from pressure.
- Keep moving and work hard off the ball to give the ball carrier an immediate option to pass.
- Attacking players should maintain width within the grid to isolate defenders.

PROGRESSION

Introduce conditions to make the drill more difficult, for example no passes above the head, players to run and touch a marker after passing and so on.

DRILL Switch relays

SKILL
Support: The execution of a switch pass must be excellent.

SETUP
- 2 balls between eight or more players
- 4 cones per grid – set up two adjacent 5 m² grids

DESCRIPTION

Players line up as shown in the diagram and work in pairs. The two players run diagonally across the grid and perform a switch as they pass each other, then run around the markers at the end of the grid and repeat the skill on the way back. The drill continues for a set period of time. Players should alternate the marker they start from after every repetition. Race the two teams to see which can perform the most switches in a minute, for example.

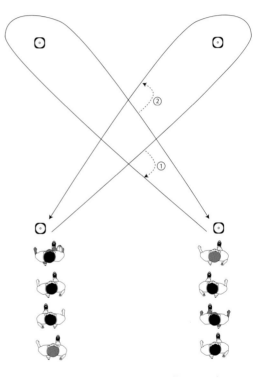

COACHING POINTS

- The support player should mirror the angle of the ball carrier for the first couple of steps before cutting across the grid.
- The ball carrier should keep the support player in his peripheral vision at all times and not turn away from him to make the pass.
- The ball carrier should deliver a pop pass, where the ball is placed up in to space instead of directed at the player.
- The support runner should time the run to hit the ball at pace.

PROGRESSION

Work a shake in to the movement (see page 15).

DRILL 2v2 attacking movement patterns

SKILL

Unit play: Movement destabilises defenders and creates attacking opportunities.

SETUP
- 1 ball between 4 or more players
- 2 cones

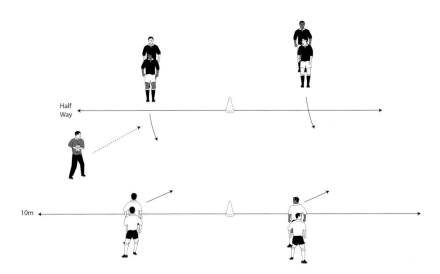

DESCRIPTION

Players line up 5 m either side of a marker at both ends of the grid, as shown in the diagram, and play in pairs. Whichever pair the coach passes the ball to become the attackers, while the pair opposite defend. The attackers try to beat the defence using the attacking movement patterns in Part One (see pages 13–24). There is no limit on width.

COACHING POINTS

- Use acceleration and dynamic changes of direction to stretch and isolate defenders.
- See the notes on each attacking movement pattern in Part One (see pages 13–24).

DRILL 3v2 teams

SKILL
Unit play: Attackers should aim to isolate and target specific defenders.

SETUP
- 1 ball between 12 or more players
- 6 cones marking out a maximum 20 m × 20 m grid

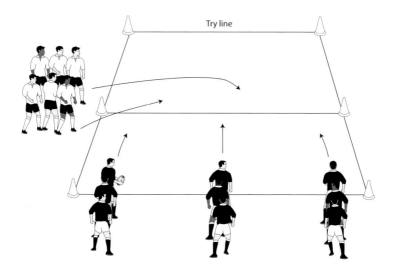

Try line

DESCRIPTION
Split the squad into two teams. The attacking team aims to score as many times as possible. The defenders work in pairs and must start from the central line and advance when the ball carrier taps the ball. The competition is timed (5 minutes).

COACHING POINTS
- Attackers should look to create a two-on-one.
- Attackers should run with pace and purpose and aim to attack individual defenders.
- Support players should accelerate in to gaps.
- Use the attacking movement patterns on pages 13–24, but scan the defence before making a call.

DRILL   3v2 continuous

SKILL
Unit play: Consistency is key – if you can beat them once, you should beat them every time.

SETUP
- 1 ball between 7 players
- 6 cones marking a 20 m² grid, ideally situated between the 10 m lines

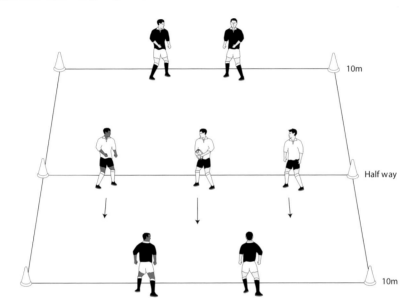

10m

Half way

10m

DESCRIPTION

Two defenders position at each end of the grid. They are allowed to advance only when the attackers cross the half-way line. Three attackers line up on the half-way line and attack alternate ends of the grid, aiming to beat the two defenders to score on the 10 m line. The players continue to attack alternate ends of the grid for a set period of time.

COACHING POINTS

- Attackers should look to create a two-on-one.
- Attackers should run with pace and purpose and aim to attack individual defenders.
- Players should communicate to regain shape and alignment following an attack.
- Use the attacking movement patterns on pages 13–24 to beat the defence.

DRILL   4v3 line-up

SKILL
Unit play: Make a decision based on the state of the defence.

SETUP
1 ball between 7 players

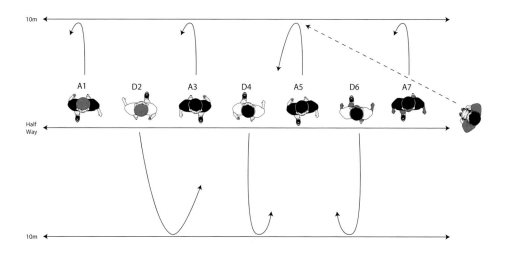

DESCRIPTION

Seven players stand 5 m apart on the half-way line. The players at positions 2, 4 and 6 are always defenders; the other four players are attackers. After every drill, the players line up randomly. The coach rolls the ball to start the drill. The attackers retrieve the ball, turn and aim to score a try on the far 10 m line. The defenders retreat a set distance (10 m line) before moving up to defend. The drill ends when the attack score or the defence tackle the ball carrier and he is unable to keep the ball alive.

COACHING POINTS

- The attack should go forwards quickly to attack the defence before they have time to organise.
- All attackers should be active in assessing the defence to help direct play and communicate to give the ball carrier options.
- Look to create two-on-ones, or use the attacking movement patterns on pages 13–24 to break the defensive line.

DRILL   4v3 link drill

SKILL
Support: The link player gives the ball carrier a quick option to clear the ball from pressure.

SETUP
- 1 ball between 7 players
- 4 cones marking out a 25 m by 15 m grid

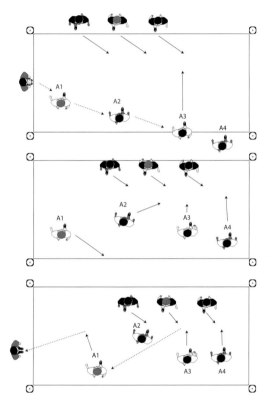

DESCRIPTION

Four attackers play against three defenders. The drill starts when the coach feeds the ball to the attack, who should try to exploit the overlap and play 'Numbers' (see pages 3–4). The defenders play with full contact and combine to prevent a try. A1 plays 'link' (see pages 7–11) and the other attackers should avoid contact and use the attacking movement patterns (see pages 13–24) to beat the defence. The aim is to either score a try or to successfully get the ball back to the coach via the link.

COACHING POINTS

- Hold the ball in both hands.
- Use the full width of the grid to isolate and stretch defenders.
- Attack as a unit of three, with support either side of the ball carrier.
- Anticipate and dynamically recoil from contact if there is no option to break through the defence.
- The link should move to a deep position inside the ball as swiftly as possible to give the ball carrier the option of a playback (see pages 40–42).

PROGRESSION

Introduce a fourth defender.

DRILL   6v4 'easy'

SKILL
Unit play: Depth of support gives the attack more chances to score.

SETUP
- 1 ball between 10 players
- 4 cones marking out a grid roughly 20 m by 30 m, played inside the 22 between the 15 m lines

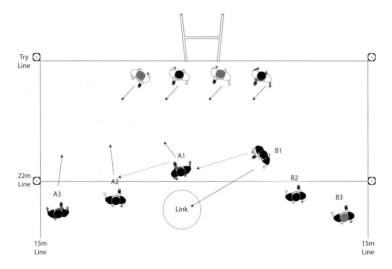

DESCRIPTION

Six attackers play against four defenders. The attackers are split into two units of three players: As and Bs. As the As attack, the Bs realign to receive the ball. One player from the Bs should move into position as a link (see pages 7–11). The attackers should avoid contact and aim to beat the defence to score over the try line using the attacking movement patterns on pages 13–24. The defenders play as a defensive line and simulate a tackle with a two-handed tag on the ball carrier. The drill is restarted after a score or a tag.

COACHING POINTS

- Use the full width of the grid to stretch the defenders.
- Commit to the attack in threes, with support on either side of the ball carrier.
- Be quick to provide the ball carrier with the 'easy' option (see pages 25–8).
- No ball-watching; work hard off the ball and get in to position early.
- See pages 7–11 for more on the link pattern. Here, six players are used instead of seven to make the drill more intensive.

9 CONTINUITY DRILLS

DRILL   Hit and spin

SKILL
Continuity: Players should aim to stay on their feet in contact and keep the ball alive.

SETUP
- 1 ball between 10 players
- 2 pads
- 4 cones marking out a 15 m × 10 m grid

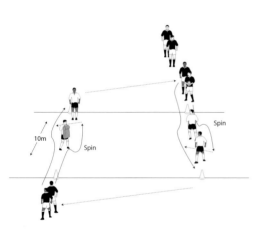

DESCRIPTION
Two players with pads stand between the markers as shown. A defender stands in front of each cone and the other players line up behind the cones. Players run in pairs: the ball carrier hits the pad and spins out of contact, then plays a two-on-one with his support player against a defender, who can only move laterally. The ball is then passed to the next pair in line and the drill continues. Change the players with pads frequently.

COACHING POINTS
- The ball carrier should keep the ball in two hands, which facilitates quicker rotation and better ball security.
- Plant the foot close to the defender and roll off the same shoulder.
- The last stride before contact should establish a wide base of support for balance.
- Sink low and drive up and forwards in the spin.
- Avoid driving the shoulder straight into the centre of the pad. Hit to the side and spin dynamically off the pad.

DRILL   Ruck review

SKILL	SETUP
Continuity: Contact should be managed in attacking units of three players.	• 1 ball between 10 players • 2 pads • 4 cones laid out as shown in the diagram below

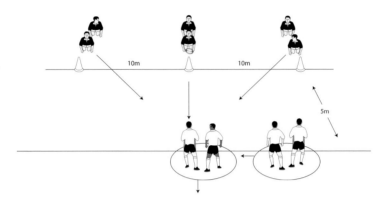

DESCRIPTION

The attacking team line up behind the cones as shown and start the drill on all fours. On the ball carrier's call, they get to their feet and the ball carrier runs into the pad, supported by the players alongside him. The defence play in pairs: one on a pad to take the initial hit, the other to contest for possession. As one pair are driven back, the next pair move on to the marker to defend against the next attacking unit. The attack aim to secure possession and pass the ball back to the next attacking unit, who start the drill again.

COACHING POINTS

- The ball carrier should transfer the ball to the arm furthest from the pad.
- On contact, the ball carrier should be aggressive with shoulder rolls and elbows to prevent the defender from getting his hands on the ball.
- The ball carrier should control the ball on the ground with two hands and use his abdominal strength to reach back and place the ball as far back as possible (see 'long place' on pages 30–31).
- Support players should achieve a low body position and get an arm under the defender to lift him up and away from the ball (see notes on 'Punch-arm', page 32).

DRILL   Truck and trailers

SKILL
Continuity: Players should manage the contact area efficiently and swiftly.

SETUP
- 2+ balls between 12+ players
- 3+ pads
- 4 cones marking out a 20 m² grid

DESCRIPTION
Groups of three players jog around the grid passing a ball between them. Pad carriers jog randomly around the grid. On the coach's whistle, the player holding the ball runs, hits a pad and goes to ground, and the support players move to secure and recycle possession. After contact, the players start passing the ball again and the drill continues.

COACHING POINTS
- The ball carrier should hit the pad with a low body position and maintain his leg drive with short powerful steps until the support player calls for him to go to ground.
- The ball carrier should show abdominal strength to perform a long place (see page 31).
- The primary support player must assume a low body position and keep his chin off his chest in contact.
- The secondary support player should instruct the primary support player to either hold over the ball or drive the defender away.

DRILL   Star running

SKILL	SETUP
Continuity: Communication should increase in contact.	• 1 ball between 3 players • 5 players with pads • 5 cones marking out a 5-point star in a 20 m² grid

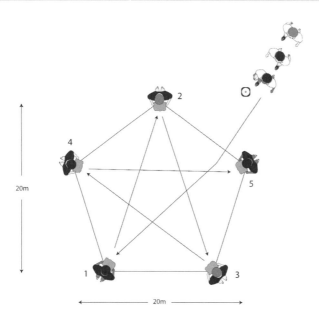

DESCRIPTION

A player with a pad stands just in front of each marker. The other players work in threes and hit each pad in order, 1–5; the ball carrier hits the pad, the second player supports in contact and the third player picks up the ball and runs to hit the next pad. Two or three attacking teams can work at once.

COACHING POINTS

- The ball carrier should maintain his foot speed in to contact.
- Ball carrier to pick a target on the pad and drive his shoulder through the contact.
- The ball carrier should hit the ground with the ball in both hands.
- Support players should communicate whether to hold over the ball or cleanout, and hit ruck with a low body height and a good body shape.

DRILL Multiple rucks

SKILL	SETUP
Continuity: Players must work hard in support.	• 1 ball between 8 players • 4 pads • 4 cones set out on the halfway line around 10 m apart

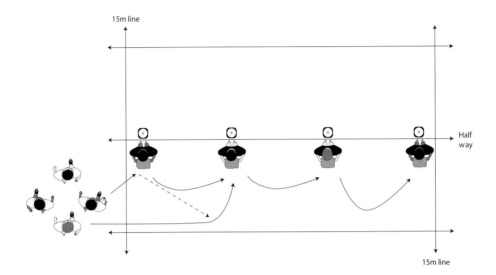

DESCRIPTION

Four players with pads stand at each cone facing the 15 m line. In fours, players perform a ruck on each of the pads: the first player hits the pad, the next player bridges and the third player passes out to the fourth player, who then hits the next pad and so on. Be sure to work both directions so players have the opportunity to hit with both shoulders and pass off both hands.

COACHING POINTS

- Players should pick a point on the pad to hit and drive the shoulder in, maintaining their speed and a low body position.
- Support players should communicate and work hard to recycle the ball quickly in defence.
- Players should maintain leg drive in contact, using short, quick steps.
- The clearing pass from the ruck should be wide and deep. After the pass, the support line should follow the line of the ball.

DRILL   Offloads

SKILL	SETUP
Continuity: The first priority in the tackle is to offload the ball.	1 ball between 3 players.

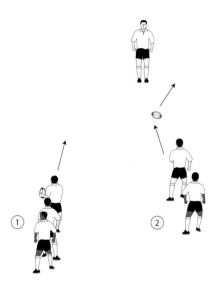

DESCRIPTION

Teams of three players spread out along the touchline. The first player runs out 5–10 m, places the ball on the ground, runs on another 5 m or so and then turns to defend. The next player runs out, picks up the ball, runs to either side of the defender and offloads in the tackle to the third player. The third player takes the ball forwards and the drill restarts. Players should aim to fit in as many repetitions as possible before they reach the other side of the field.

COACHING POINTS

- Carry the ball in both hands to withstand the impact of the tackle.
- Keep the arms free above the level of the tackle.
- Before hitting the ground, pop the ball in to the space for the support player.
- The support player should accelerate in to the space created by the ball carrier's movement.

DRILL   Race for roles

SKILL	SETUP
Continuity: Speed is an essential ingredient in support play.	• 1 ball between 6 players • 1 pad • 4 cones marking out a 20 m × 10 m grid

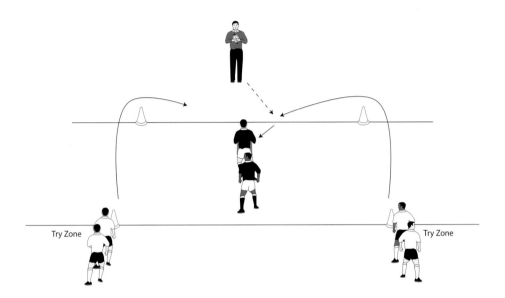

Try Zone

Try Zone

DESCRIPTION

Two defenders stand in the middle of the grid, one holding a pad and the other positioned directly behind to contest possession. Attackers run in fours, two from each side of the grid. The coach passes to the first attacker around his marker, who then proceeds to hit the pad. The other attackers communicate to manage the ruck and clear the ball. The clearing pass should be long, so the first receiver off the ruck scores outside the markers.

COACHING POINTS

- The ball carrier should maintain foot speed in to and during contact.
- Transfer the ball to the arm furthest from the pad and be aggressive with shoulder rolls and elbows on contact.
- Support players should be quick to communicate so that the ball is secured in contact and cleared from pressure as swiftly as possible.

DRILL 1v1 with support

SKILL

Continuity: The ball carrier must stay strong in contact.

SETUP

- 1 ball between 5 players
- 4 cones marking out a 10 m² grid

DESCRIPTION

The defender stands in the middle of the grid with an attacker on each side of the grid, as shown in the diagram. The defender passes to any attacker, who then aims to evade the defender and get to the other side of the grid. If contact is made, the other three attackers move in to the grid to support, and must enter the tackle contest from behind the ball in an onside position. The defender should aim to get to his feet after the tackle and contest possession.

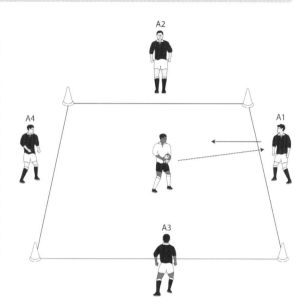

COACHING POINTS

- Use a fend and forearm to keep the defender away from the ball.
- Aim to offload in the tackle, or perform a long place if tackled to ground (see page 31).
- The secondary support player should call to direct the primary support player.
- The clearing pass from the tackle area should be long, so the first receiver should align outside the borders of the grid.

PROGRESSION

Advance the drill by adding another defender.

DRILL 4v2

SKILL
Continuity: Players must communicate to make sure all support roles are filled quickly.

SETUP
- 1 ball between 6 players
- 6 cones placed 10 m apart, as shown in the diagram

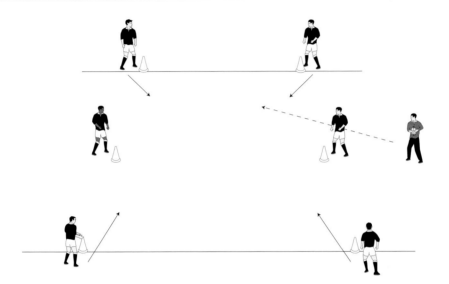

DESCRIPTION

One player stands on each marker. The coach starts the drill by rolling the ball in to the middle of four of the players, who become the attacking team. The two players at the opposite end of the grid move to defend as soon as the coach rolls the ball. The attacking team aim to beat the defence and score a try at the opposite end of the grid.

COACHING POINTS

- The attackers in front of the ball must get back to support.
- The ball carrier should transfer the ball to the arm furthest from the tackler and use shoulder rolls and elbows to prevent a turnover in the tackle.
- All support players must start communicating to direct play immediately.
- The primary support player must match the height of the defender in the tackle contest and get an arm under the defender to prevent a turnover (see notes on 'Punch-arm', page 32).

DRILL   Hit and link

SKILL	SETUP
Continuity: Teams should aim to recycle the ball quickly in contact.	• 1 ball between 11 players • 4 pads

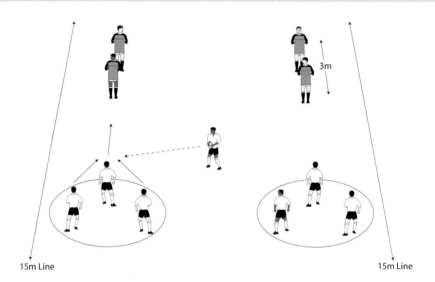

15m Line   15m Line

DESCRIPTION

The drill takes place between the 15 m lines up the length of the pitch. A link player passes the ball between two attacking units of three players each, who aim to recycle the ball and then pass it back to the link player. Two pad carriers defend against each unit, one about 3 m behind the other. The attacking players rotate positions within their unit.

COACHING POINTS

- The ball carrier should try to sidestep the first pad or hit it and roll off, then drive on the second pad until support players call for him to go to ground.
- Maintain a low body position and leg drive in contact.
- Perform a tunnel-ball or long place (see pages 30–31).
- The primary support player should hit contact with a low body position, with his shoulders above his hips and his chin off his chest for safety.
- When bridging over the ball, players must be self-supporting and not leaning on the tackled player.

DRILL   1v1 tracking

SKILL	SETUP
Individual defence: Tracking determines the success of the tackle.	• 2 players • 4 cones marking out a 5 m² grid

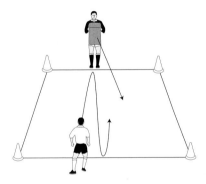

DESCRIPTION

A defender and a pad carrier stand at opposite ends of the grid. The defender runs and touches the pad, then returns to the line he started on. As soon as the defender gets back to his start line, the pad carrier moves forwards through the grid and tries to reach the other side. The defender should aim to make good shoulder contact on the pad and drive the pad backwards and out of the grid. Players should swap roles after a specific number of repetitions.

COACHING POINTS

- Move forwards off the line quickly to cut down time and space.
- Approach slightly to one side of the pad carrier, allowing him only one direction in which to run.
- Keep the head to the side for safety.
- Plant the lead foot close in to the pad and make firm contact with the shoulder (see pages 55–6).
- Wrap with the arms and use strong leg drive to keep the shoulder nailed to the opponent and drive him backwards.

PROGRESSION

Advance the drill by making the grid bigger.

DRILL   Crossover tackles

SKILL
Individual defence: Every player must have solid one-on-one defence.

SETUP
- 4 balls between 5 players
- 4 cones marking out a 10 m² grid

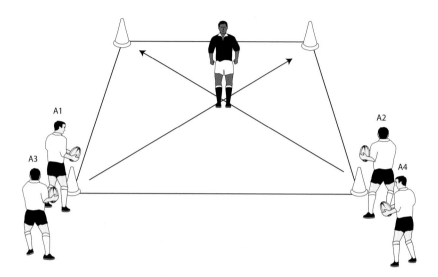

DESCRIPTION

A defender stands in the middle of the grid and the attackers, each with a ball, line up behind the markers at one end of the grid as shown in the diagram. The attackers run diagonally through the grid in turn, alternating from each marker, and the defender aims to tackle them. When all the ball carriers have run through the grid to their opposite markers, they then return in order. The defender continues for a set time or a specific number of tackles, then the players swap roles.

COACHING POINTS

- The defender should approach slightly to one side of the ball carrier.
- Plant the lead foot as close to the ball carrier as possible.
- Make firm contact with the shoulder around the level of the ball.
- Keep the head to the side for safety.
- Wrap with the arms and use leg drive to force the ball carrier back out of the grid.

DRILL   Approach drill

SKILL
Individual defence: The ball carrier should only have one direction in which he can run.

SETUP
• 1 ball between 2 players
• 5 cones marking out a 10 m × 5 m grid

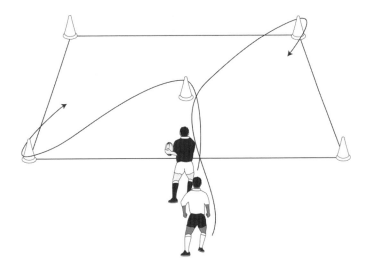

DESCRIPTION

Two players line up in front of the grid as shown in the diagram. The player in front carries a ball. Both players run to the centre marker; the ball carrier then chooses a corner marker to run around and the defender must run around the marker diagonally opposite. The defender then aims to tackle the ball carrier or drive him out of the grid.

COACHING POINTS

• The defender should move forwards quickly to take up the attacker's space.
• Keep the attacker on the outside shoulder and continue cutting off the angle to narrow his space.
• Use footwork to get in tight to the attacker and make firm contact using the shoulder.
• Be aggressive in contact and use leg drive to keep the shoulder nailed to the attacker.

DRILL   Defend-a-man

SKILL
Individual defence: The ball carrier can be controlled by using a considered approach.

SETUP
- 1 ball between 2+ players
- 4 cones marking out a 10 m² grid

DESCRIPTION

Divide the players into two teams, attackers and defenders, and line them up facing each other at opposite ends of the grid. The two players at the front of each line run towards each other and the ball carrier pops a pass to his opponent. They both then race around the markers and enter the grid. The defender aims to make a tackle and stop the attacker scoring.

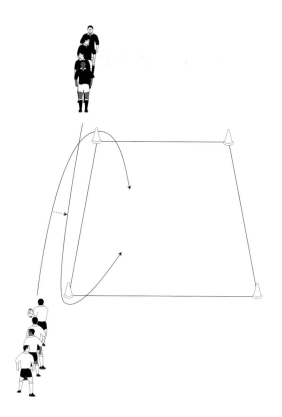

COACHING POINTS

- The defender should move forwards quickly to take up the space.
- Keep the attacker on the outside shoulder and continue cutting off the angle to narrow his space.
- Get in close to the attacker and make firm shoulder contact.
- Use leg drive in the tackle to keep the shoulder nailed to the attacker.

DRILL   1v1 pressure

SKILL
Individual defence: The defender must cut down the time and space of the attacker.

SETUP
- 1 ball between 2+ players
- 8 cones marking out four goals on a 15 m² grid (see diagram)

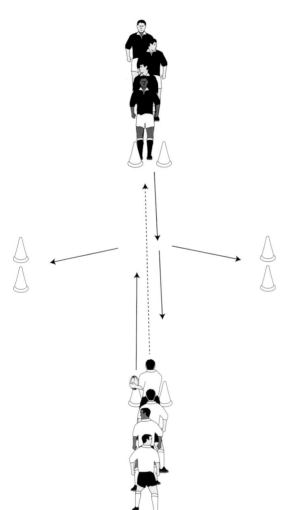

DESCRIPTION
Two lines of players stand at opposite ends of the grid behind two of the goals. The drill starts when the player at the front of one line passes the ball to the player at the front of the other line. The receiver becomes the attacker and tries to score by running through any of the three goals ahead of him. The passer becomes the defender and aims to tackle the ball carrier to ground or drive him out of the grid.

COACHING POINTS
- The defender should move forwards off the line quickly to cut down the time and space available to the ball carrier.
- Push up on the inside shoulder, giving the attacker only one direction to attack (see pages 49–50).
- Keep on the balls of the feet to be able to react better to directional changes.
- Get the feet in close to the ball carrier to make the tackle.

DRILL   Line running

SKILL

Line defence: It takes practice to move as a line.

SETUP

- 10+ players
- 5 cones laid out along the whole pitch as shown in the diagram
- 5 pads

DESCRIPTION

Five defenders form a defensive wall on their try line and five pad carriers line up opposite them. The defenders hit the pads, then 'pancake' (drop to their front, flip on to their back, flip back on to their front, then jump up to their feet). During the pancake, the pad carriers run to their next position. The pad carriers should also keep a defensive line as they move. The defenders then slide across field to hit their pad. The drill continues for the full length of the pitch.

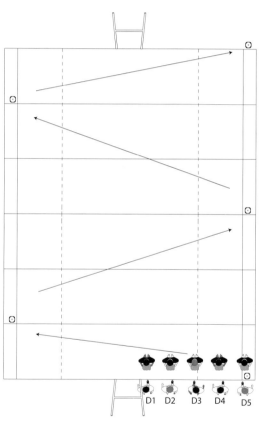

COACHING POINTS

- Players should stay tight and allow no gaps to open up as the line moves across the field.

- The player leading the slide (D1 going left; D5 going right) should sprint to force all players to work hard to maintain inside cover.

- The last player in the slide (D5 going left; D1 going right) should call up the line to keep it flat, not diagonal.

- Communication throughout the drill should be constant.

DRILL   Figure of eight

SKILL

Line defence: The defensive wall must stay intact.

SETUP

- 6 players
- 8 cones set up on the try line and 22 m line, as shown in the diagram

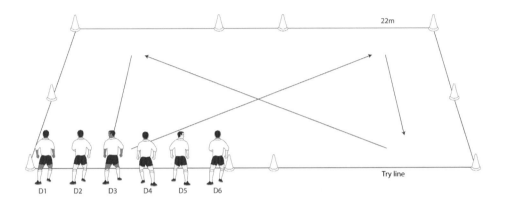

DESCRIPTION

Six players stand around 5 m apart to form a defensive wall on the try line. They move as a line in a figure of eight – up and across field from the try line to the 22 m, back pedal to the try line, up and across the other way, then finish with a back pedal to the starting position. Three teams can work at the same time. The drill continues for a set time or set number of repetitions.

COACHING POINTS

- Players should move together to prevent gaps opening up in the defensive wall.
- The player leading the slide (D6 going right; D1 going left) should sprint to force all players to work hard to maintain inside cover.
- All players should push up and across to keep the defensive wall flat.
- Inside players should communicate constantly to outside players.

DRILL   Tackle relay

SKILL

Line defence: The defence must number up from the outside to prevent overlaps.

SETUP

- 16 players
- 4 tackle bags
- 6 cones laid out as shown in the diagram

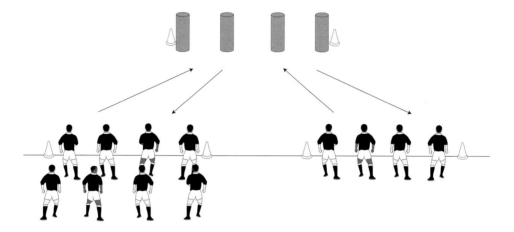

DESCRIPTION

In teams of four, players stand about 5 m apart. Four players holding tackle bags position 5 m away. The first team in line move up through the markers, tackle the bags and then aim to keep their defensive line as they pass through the other cones. They then tap the next team, who restart the drill, and the relay continues. Change bag holders frequently.

COACHING POINTS

- Players should number up from the outside to cover all the bags. The bags should be numbered depending on their position from the outside: when approaching from the left the bag on the far right is 'last', the bag inside that one is '2', then '3', and finally '4' is the bag on the far left; and vice versa when approaching from the right. Players should nominate their bag: 'I've got last', 'I've got 2' and so on.

- Players should get their feet in close to the bag, hit with the outside shoulder and wrap with the arms.

- Players should react quickly after the tackle to re-establish the defensive line.

DRILL   Slide

SKILL	SETUP
Line defence: Defenders must be careful not to over-track past the inside shoulder.	• 11 players • 6 pads

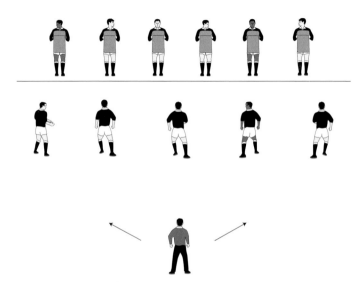

DESCRIPTION

Five players form a defensive line facing six pad carriers. The coach stands behind the defenders and directs the pad carriers, who move laterally left or right. The defenders follow the pads left and right. On the coach's signal, the pad carriers run forwards and the defenders hit them. After the hit, the defenders drop to the ground and do a pancake (see page 116). The pad carriers and coach then change places and the drill continues with the defenders playing in the opposite direction.

COACHING POINTS

- The defence should number up as the pad carriers move: if they move to the left, the defenders should leave the pad carrier on the far right, and vice versa.
- Constant nomination of who has which bag is essential.
- Defenders should always keep the pad on their outside shoulder.
- Use footwork to get in close to the pad and make firm shoulder contact with leg drive in the hit.

DRILL   Post-tackle work rate

SKILL
Line defence: The defence must be quick to reorganise following a tackle.

SETUP
- 1 ball between 15 players
- 5 pads
- 4 cones set out on the halfway and 10 m lines, as shown in the diagram

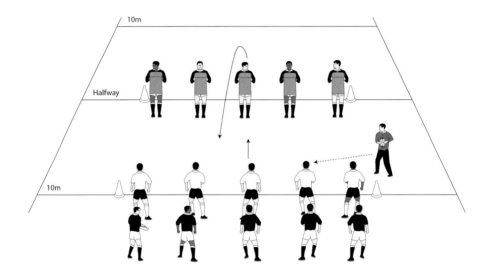

DESCRIPTION

Five defenders form a line on the 10 m line facing five pad carriers on the halfway line. Five attackers stand behind the defenders. On the coach's signal, the defenders move up as a line and hit the pads. They then turn and defend the attacking line, who are fed a ball by the coach. The attackers can use as much width as they want. The drill continues until a tackle is made.

COACHING POINTS

- Defenders should communicate to establish the defensive wall quickly.
- The defence should keep moving forwards to take up the space and apply pressure.
- Defenders should keep their opponent on their outside shoulder.
- Each defender should stay tight to the player outside him as he moves across the pitch to close gaps and cover the inside.

DRILL   Turnover

SKILL
Unit defence: The aim of the defence is always to regain possession.

SETUP
- 1 ball between 3+ players
- 6 cones marking out a 10 m² grid and the starting position for each team, as shown in the diagram

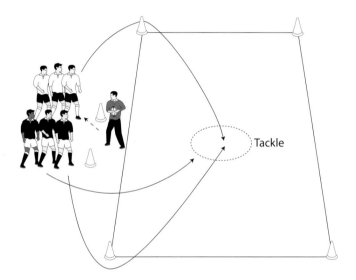

Tackle

DESCRIPTION

Two teams of players line up facing the grid. The coach passes to one of the players, who runs around a marker and enters the grid to attack. The player in the other team runs around the opposite marker and enters the grid to defend. As soon as the two players make contact, the next player from the defending team runs straight into the grid and tries to steal the ball.

COACHING POINTS

- The first defender should pick a target area to hit on the ball carrier and drive his shoulder through that target.
- The inside cover defender should assist in the tackle if the ball carrier is still moving forwards, but must stay on his feet.
- When contesting the ball, stay in a low body position and step over the ball to pick it up.
- Keep the chin off the chest for safety.

DRILL   Live switch

SKILL	SETUP
Unit defence: Defenders must be prepared to cover changes of direction.	• 1 ball between 4+ players • 6 cones marking out a 15 m × 10 m grid

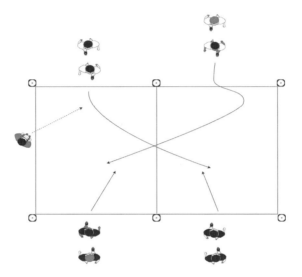

DESCRIPTION

Players line up in pairs at opposite ends of the grid. Whichever pair the coach passes the ball to become the attackers, and the pair opposite defend. The two attackers aim to beat the defence with a switch (see pages 16–18); the two defenders aim to stop the attack and cover the switch.

COACHING POINTS

- The outside defender must stay on his man and not get drawn in by the ball carrier running towards him.
- Communication is essential: the outside defender should call as soon as he sees his opponent running for the switch and the inside defender should be quick to react to the call.
- Both defenders must hold their channel. Dig the heels in to the ground to stop momentum, then immediately move forwards to make the tackle.

DRILL   Covering the loop

SKILL
Unit defence: Communication plays a huge part in defending a loop.

SETUP
- 2 balls between 8+ players
- 2 cones 10 m apart

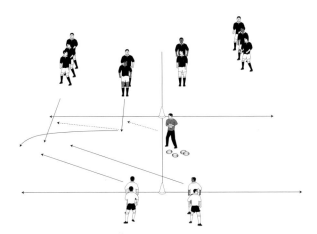

DESCRIPTION
This is a two-on-two drill where the attack try to beat the defence with a loop (see pages 20–22). The attacking players line up in pairs on either side of a marker, and two pairs of defenders stand on the opposite side of the grid. The coach feeds the ball to an attacking pair to start the drill. The defenders have to react quickly and slide to cover the loop.

COACHING POINTS
- Defenders should start nominating their man early, and keep communicating as the loop is performed.
- The outside defender has to slide across to cover the looping player, while the inside defender moves to cover the ball carrier.
- Both defenders must be careful not to over-track past the player they are marking.
- The defenders should close down the ball carrier as quickly as possible.

PROGRESSION
The coach can feed a ball to attackers on both sides of the grid at once to increase the intensity of the drill.

DRILL   3v3 pads

SKILL

Unit defence: Defenders must aim to exert pressure as an organised unit.

SETUP
- 6 players
- 6 cones marking out 2 adjacent grids, each measuring 15 m × 10 m
- 3 pads

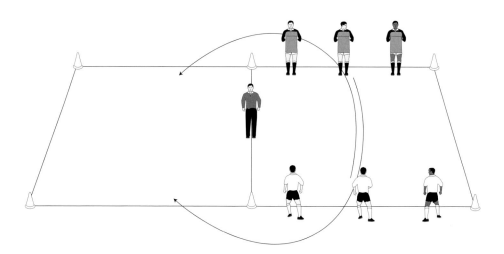

DESCRIPTION

Two teams of three players face each other across a grid. One team have pads, the other team are defenders. On the coach's call, the teams run past each other and enter the adjacent grid for three-on-three defence. The pad carriers are attackers and try to evade the defenders to progress through the grid. The defenders aim to cover all the pad carriers and drive them out of the grid.

COACHING POINTS

- The defenders should establish the defensive wall and nominate an attacker early.
- Defenders should advance as a line quickly to cut down the time and space available to the attacking players.
- Defenders should keep the pad on their outside shoulder.
- Get the feet in close for the hit and maintain leg drive in contact.
- Hook the lead leg of the attacking player to eliminate his power and facilitate a drive.

DRILL   Inside cover

SKILL

Unit defence: The defence must move as a line, not as individuals.

SETUP

- 1 ball between 11 players
- 12 cones set out as shown in the diagram

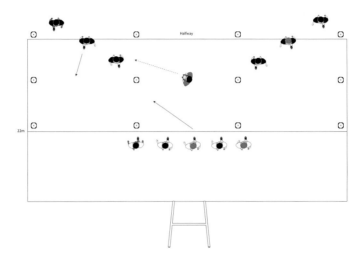

DESCRIPTION

The full width of the field is used for this drill. Five defenders start between two markers on the 22 m line. This is their base, which they return to whenever the coach has the ball. Six attackers split into two attacking units of three players (As and Bs) who take turns to attack in marked grids on either side of the coach. The two units do not interact, so the coach dictates the speed of the drill. Whichever way the coach passes, the defence slide across to cover. The defenders aim to prevent a line-break and force a turnover. Defenders work for a set period of time (60/90/120 seconds).

COACHING POINTS

- All defenders number up from the outside and nominate an attacker.
- Defenders should move up and across to take up the space.
- The defence should communicate to outside players to maintain inside cover.
- Keep the opponent on the outside shoulder and be careful not to over-track.
- Get the feet in close to the attacker to ensure firm shoulder contact is made.

DRILL   Raiders

SKILL
Conditioned game: Attacking with urgency increases pressure on the defence.

SETUP
- 2 balls between 10 players
- 12 cones marking out a 20 m × 30 m grid, split into thirds, as shown in the diagram.

DESCRIPTION

Players are in two teams of five, with one ball per team. Each team can allocate any number of players to attack or defend. The aim is to score a try before the opposite team. Defenders aim to make a two-handed tag on the ball carrier, which forces 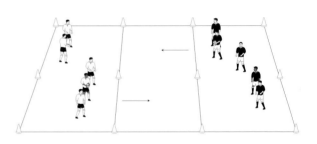 the opposing attackers to retreat and start again from their third of the field. Attackers must retreat if they pass forwards or drop the ball.

COACHING POINTS

- All players must communicate to coordinate attacking and defensive patterns.
- The attackers should use the full width of the grid to isolate the defenders and create two-on-one situations.
- The defenders should identify who they are marking and nominate their man as early as possible.

PROGRESSION

Advance the game by adding more players to each team.

DRILL   4v4 offloads

SKILL
Conditioned game: The quality of the run will determine the success of the offload.

SETUP
- 1 ball between 8 players
- 10 cones marking out a 30 m × 40 m grid

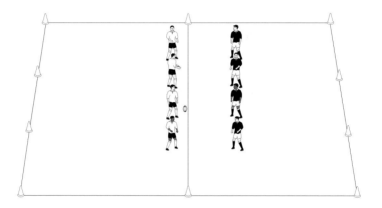

DESCRIPTION

Players are in two teams of four, one attacking and one defending. The game begins with a tap penalty in the centre of the grid. The defenders must make a two-handed touch on the ball carrier and then block his attempts to offload the ball. The ball carrier should not stop dead when touched, but use momentum to get behind the defensive line to offload the ball. If he cannot offload without delay, he must take a quick tap and pass the ball. If an offload is unsuccessful or knocked to the ground by the defence, the defence win the ball. All attackers must be over the try line before a try can be scored. The scoring team keep the ball and play out from the try line.

COACHING POINTS

- Run the attacking movement patterns on pages 13–24.
- Attack the space between defenders and always aim to get behind the defensive line.
- Offloads should only be given if there is absolute certainty they will go to hand, otherwise stop and take a quick tap.
- Support players must communicate and work hard off the ball.
- The defenders must cover insides and compress when the ball carrier makes a break to prevent him from offloading the ball.

DRILL   Escape

SKILL
Conditioned game: Dynamic changes of pace and angle will help you isolate and beat defenders.

SETUP
- 1 ball between 10 players
- 14 cones marking out a 20 m × 30 m outer grid and a 10 m × 20 m inner grid

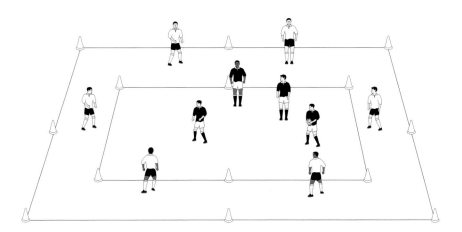

DESCRIPTION

Four attackers play against six defenders. The defenders can move anywhere in the outer grid, but must not enter the inner grid. The attackers work together to get the ball outside both of the grids. They can pass the ball in any direction when inside the inner grid, but are not allowed to pass the ball forwards when they attack the outer grid. The defenders must work together to shut down the attackers and make a touch on the ball carrier. If the ball carrier gets touched in the outer grid, he changes places with the defender who made the touch.

COACHING POINTS

- Encourage the attackers to plan and work together to isolate defenders and create two-on-one situations.
- The attackers should change direction sharply to attack space.
- The ball carrier should pull back to avoid getting touched, and be quick to move the ball to a player in a position to sustain the attack.
- The drill teaches defenders to stay alert, communicate constantly and coordinate with the players on either side to cover attacks.

DRILL   Turnaround touch

SKILL	SETUP
Conditioned game: Attackers should keep scanning the defence for opportunities.	• 1 ball between 14 players • 1 cone

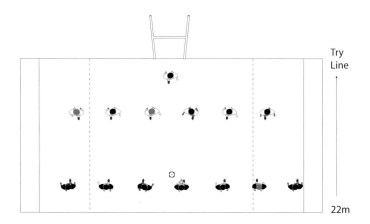

Try Line

22m

DESCRIPTION

This is a 7v7 game played in the 22 m area. The game starts with a tap penalty on a centre marker. The defenders start 10 m back. A defender must make a two-handed touch on the ball carrier, and then run back to the try line before re-entering the game. After the touch, the ball carrier must hit the ground and place the ball. The primary support player must bridge and hold over the ball, and a second support player then plays the ball.

If a try is scored, the defending team run to the halfway line and back and then continue to defend. If the attack make a mistake or commit an offence, the attackers and defenders change places and the game resumes immediately. The attack has five touches to score.

COACHING POINTS

- Use the attacking movement patterns on pages 13–24 to beat the defence.
- The attackers should aim to recycle the ball quickly through vocal and coordinated support play.
- Deep alignment is essential to exploit the space.
- The defence need to compress when a touch is made and must work hard to maintain the defensive line.
- The sweeper should communicate to keep the defensive line intact.

DRILL 5v4 strike

SKILL
Conditioned game: Width stretches and creates holes in the defence.

SETUP
- 1 ball between 9 players
- 10 cones marking out a 30 m × 40 m grid

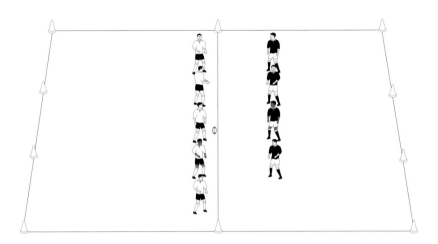

DESCRIPTION

Five attackers play against four defenders. The game begins with a tap penalty in the centre. The game is played like Rugby League, so if the ball carrier is held or put to ground in a tackle, he must get to his feet and roll the ball through his legs to restart play. The defenders must retreat 5 m from the roll-ball. The attacking team are allowed four roll-balls to score. After the fifth tackle, the ball carrier joins the opposition in attack. After the turnover, play is restarted with a roll-ball. The scorer changes teams after a try is scored and restarts the game immediately with a quick tap on the try line.

COACHING POINTS

- The first receiver off the roll-ball sets the depth for the team.
- Use width and the attacking movement patterns on pages 13–24 to stretch the defence.
- Look to keep the ball alive in the tackle.
- Aim to tackle above or as close to the level of the ball as possible to prevent an offload.
- The defenders must cover insides and compress when the ball carrier makes a break to cover offloads to support runners.

INDEX